The Computer Book of Lists and First Computer Almanack

EDMUND C. BERKELEY

Editor and Publisher
Computers and People magazine
Newtonville, Massachusetts 02160

A Reston Computer Group Book
Reston Publishing Company, Inc.
A Prentice-Hall Company
Reston, Virginia

Library of Congress Cataloging in Publication Data

Berkeley, Edmund Callis.
    The computer book of lists and computer almanack.

    "A Reston Computer Group book."
    Bibliography: p.
    Includes index.
    1. Electronic data processing. 2. Computers. 3. Lists
I. Title.
QA76.B39 1984   001.64   84-11520
ISBN 0-8359-0865-8
ISBN 0-8359-0864-X (pbk.)

DEDICATION

To all those persons and organizations
from prehistory to the present
who have taught me and helped me
to find the information reported in this volume.

10 9 8 7 6 5 4 3 2 1

PRINTED IN THE UNITED STATES OF AMERICA

Contents

Chapter 11: COMPUTERS AND LOGIC, BOOLEAN ALGEBRA, FALLACIES, ... • 97

Preface: Lists

- Computer-Related Lists
- The Pen and the Sword
- Not Only Number Crunchers
- The Variety of Intellectual Thinking Open to Computers
- Errors, Changes, Corrections, Updating

COMPUTER-RELATED LISTS

For more than five thousand years, lists of useful information gathered by many authors (real, legendary, or mythical) have been assembled into:

symbols	commandments
incantations	calendars
codes	almanacs
syllabaries	sets of tables
alphabets	sets of formulas, and
	so on.

Even since 1960 the lists (sequences) of protein molecules on the helical strands of nucleic acids, the programs that guide and control the biochemical growth and organization of living systems, have been recognized. We ourselves are "computers."

Lists are now properly seen as one of the most fundamental aspects of nature, man, mathematics, and computers. Certainly lists are more important now than the study and knowledge of classical hieroglyphic writing or the nomenclature of newly discovered insects in Patagonia.

Because computers and data processing have expanded to a phenomenal extent since the early 1940's, the years of the first operating modern automatic computers, it is now appropriate to publish a computer book of lists for the computer field.

The method behind this book was finding, observing, collecting, originating, and deducing lists of computer-related information, lists that are factual, useful, and understandable. Computer-related information needs wide interpretation, to include both distantly-related and closely-related information. An amazing phenomenon of computers is that new areas for application and new impulses for understanding computers are continually erupting.

But the gathering together of factual and useful lists does not exclude some other properties of at least some lists: humorous, entertaining, puzzling, thought-provoking, mind-stimulating.

THE PEN AND THE SWORD

In 1944, one of the first of the automatic computers began to pour out useful numbers (trajectory calculations for World War II guns). This machine was the Harvard IBM Automatic Sequence Controlled Calculator, called the Mark I, situated in the Computation Laboratory of Professor Howard H. Aiken in Cambridge, Mass. I arrived there at age 36 on Navy assignment in August 1945, and found it to be an exciting machine expressing one of the most extraordinary promises for the future of mankind that I had ever expected to see. Soon thereafter I wrote one of the first books in the computer field, *Giant Brains, or Machines That Think,* which was published by John Wiley and Sons in 1949.

In that book, in Chapter 11, "The Future: Machines that Think and What They Might do for Men," occur these paragraphs (written more than 30 years ago):

> The pen is mightier than the sword, it is often said. And if this is true, then the pen with a motor may be mightier than the sword with a motor.
>
> In the Middle Ages, there were few kinds of weapons, and it was easy for a man to protect himself against most of them by wearing armor. As gunpowder came into use, a man could no longer carry the weight of armor that would protect him, and so armor was given up. But in 1917, armor equipped with a motor and carrying the man and his weapons, came back into service—as the tank....
>
> We can even imagine what new machinery for handling information may some day become: a small pocket instrument that we carry around with us, talking to it whenever we need to, and either storing information in it or receiving information from it.
>
> Thus the brain with a motor will guide and advise the man just as the armor with a motor carries and protects him.

NOT ONLY NUMBER CRUNCHERS

In those days most people thought of computers as number crunchers. But I had been interested in Boolean algebra and symbolic logic since 1927. I had realized that the presence or absence of an X punch in an IBM punch card was an expression of a truth value in logic, true or false, yes or no, T or F, 1 or 0, a binary digit. It was perfectly clear to me that all symbolic expressions of numbers, data, files, formulas, words, ideas, systems of ideas, etc., in mathematics or any other branch of knowledge, would one day be handled by these machines. And if a human brain of chemical constituents, such as carbon, hydrogen, oxygen, nitrogen..., could handle any ideas, then a mechanical or electrical or electronic brain could also handle any ideas. So the promise of these marvelous machines, "artificial intelligence," was perfectly clear.

Every thought thinkable and unthinkable can be "thought" by these machines, giant brains or miniature brains giant in power. All the thoughts of humanity are as eligible to be thought by these machines as they are by men and women—except that the machines inevitably think far more quickly and far more correctly. There is no subject anywhere in any branch of knowledge that cannot be dealt with by these machines.

But duplicating the other remarkable properties of a human being, it seems to me, will not come quickly. One of these properties is man's generalized body, capable of a great variety of sensing, behaving, and acting. Another property is man's animal brain (the animal brain is not the primate brain), with over 600 million years of evolution and adaptation. This brain has the capacity to deal with an environment, a world, and in less than a quarter second recognize what is or is not food, what is or is not danger, what is or is not means for reproducing the species. A third property is the remarkable capacity of a young child (age 2 to 7 or thereabouts) to learn something like 20,000 words and ideas, merely from being raised in a caring family and a hospitable society, and later (by something like age 21) 200,000 words and ideas.

The present name for this area of assisting humanity is robotics. Although much design and work is in progress, I believe most robots will be one-armed, one-eyed, will contain motors, gears, and wheels (not the analogs of muscles), and will be much unlike human beings for a long time to come.

THE VARIETY OF INTELLECTUAL THINKING OPEN TO COMPUTERS

In this book of lists, we show a great variety of the intellectual thinking that is open to these machines, and to people who think about these machines, both in computer applications that have happened so far and in computer applications that lie far ahead in the future and can still hardly be dreamed of.

This *Computer Almanac* needs to be as wide-ranging as the thoughts of humanity over the centuries. For we must never forget the lists of the lessons of history and the lists of principles of common sense, wisdom, and science gathered during more than 5000 years of human history.

If mankind does not come to grips with the problems of survival over the thousands of millennia that lie in the future, mankind will become just another one of the extinct species of life, like the dodo, the passenger pigeon, and the dinosaurs. In fact, as Jonathan Schell in *The Fate of the Earth* points out, if a nuclear holocaust arrives (the only possible reason on a geological time scale being nuclear weapons used by human beings), then the world of survivors if any will be "a republic of cockroaches and grass."

ERRORS, CHANGES, CORRECTIONS, UPDATING

It is certain that corrections of errors and mistakes, and changes, improvements, and updating for this volume will be needed. I shall be very grateful for all reporting of errors and changes.

The computer field of:

number processing
data processing
word processing
idea processing
robot programming

and much more besides, is a fascinating enterprise.

It might even turn out to be a major gateway to a future garden earth instead of a radioactive dying planet.

Newtonville, MA 02160   Edmund C. Berkeley
November, 1983   Editor, *Computers and People*

Introduction: More on Lists

- The Relevance of Lists
- The X-Y Table
- The Punctuation " / " (one space, slash, one space)
- The Number of Items in a List
- Counting the Number of Items in a List
- The Department of "Computers and People": CACBOL
- Forms of Writing which are Essentially Lists
- Advantages of Lists
- Lists of Great Value
- Grades for Measuring Knowledge of a Person
- Ways of Disguising Information
- Definitions of the Word "Almanac"

THE RELEVANCE OF LISTS

Some lists last forever. Others are valid only for a short time, which may range from a day or less to a lifetime or more.

Some lists are complete. For other lists, no matter how much effort is invested in gathering information, the lists will remain incomplete.

Almost all lists are culture-dependent. They are interesting, important, and worth thinking about, only if the culture (the customs, environment, wants, needs) of the person reading the list is relevant.

THE X-Y TABLE

A great many lists are in the form of an X-Y table: if X is given, Y is determined.

In assembling and printing the lists in this volume, many compromises were necessary. For example, a list in two columns (a left-hand column such as X and a right-hand column such as Y) is quite dependent on the number of characters required to express X, and those required for Y. If X takes 10 characters and Y takes 3 characters, on the average, we can print very readably as follows:

Language	Number of Speakers (millions)
Mandarin	690
English	380
Russian	259
Spanish	238

But if X takes 25 characters, and Y takes several lines, then a sensible, compact, and readable style for printing is as follows:

Joseph Jacquard (1752–1834) / machinery
   for weaving intricate designs in tapestries on looms, using punched cards
   with holes for selection of needles bearing different threads

THE PUNCTUATION " / " (ONE SPACE, SLASH, ONE SPACE)

The slash with a space on each side (" / ") represents (stands for) the vertical line often separating two columns in a table. This slash convention produces less confusion than other punctuation marks such as comma, semicolon, or colon, which have many other duties.

THE NUMBER OF ITEMS IN A LIST

There is a virtue in stating the number of items in a list, a practice much observed in this volume. A person reading the list is reminded of two ideas. The first idea is that the list may be (and often is) incomplete, and the second idea is that no claim or promise is being given by the list-compiler that the list is complete.

Even so simple an idea as the number of letters in a standard alphabet can change. The French alphabet only in the last century has come to include K and W. The English alphabet around the 1400's did not distinguish between I and J nor between U and W (the name "double-you" is a clue over 400 years old).

COUNTING THE NUMBER OF ITEMS IN A LIST

In some of the lists presented here, the items are gathered from time to time under subheadings. For example:

8 TOPICS OF A COURSE "BASIC: A COMPUTER LANGUAGE FOR MANAGERS"

Executive Computing:
  Problem solving
  Planning
  Forecasting
  Database systems

Programming Fundamentals:
  The mindless computer
  Sequence, decision, and iteration
  Computer languages
  BASIC

Are there 8 or 10 topics? Perhaps arbitrarily, we count 8 topics, not 10. The two subheadings are not to be included logically in the count.

THE DEPARTMENT OF "COMPUTERS AND PEOPLE": CACBOL

Since 1978 we have been publishing lists of computer-related information in a department of the magazine *Computers and People* (formerly *Computers and Automation*). Many (but not all) of the lists here have previously appeared in this magazine department. New developments, new editions of old lists, and presentation of new lists are planned for forthcoming issues of *Computers and People*. The department is named "Instalments of the Computer Almanac and Computer Book of Lists" (or briefly "CACBOL").

15 CATEGORIES OF STYLES OF WRITING WHICH ARE ESSENTIALLY LISTS AND COLLECTIONS

bibliography / a list of references or works (from Greek "biblio" book and "graphy" writing)

textbook / a collection of the important facts and information on a certain subject

table / a list of logarithms, measures, numbers, etc., usually displayed in columns

dictionary / a list of words and phrases with their explanations or translations (from Latin "dictio" speaking)

thesaurus / a gathering of synonyms (from Greek "thesauros" treasure)

glossary / a gathering of words in a special field (from Greek "glossa" tongue)

magazine / a collection of various information (from Arabic "makhzan" storehouse)

journal / a collection of articles in a certain field (from French "journal" daily)

newspaper / a collection of news, articles, etc., issued from time to time.

almanac / a collection of astronomical data and much other information (from Arabic "almanakh" almanac)

quotations / a book of quotations, proverbs, maxims, famous phrases, etc.

anthology / a gathering of poems, epigrams, stories,...(from Greek "anthos" flower and "logia" collecting, together garland)

encyclopedia / a collection of information on all or certain branches of knowledge (from Greek "enkyklios paidea" general education)

algorithm / a rule of procedure for solving a mathematical problem that frequently involves repetition of an operation (from Arabic "al-Khuwarizmi", Arab mathematician c. 825 AD)

program / a brief outline of the order to be pursued or the subjects to be embraced (from Greek "pro" before and "graphein" to write)

8 ADVANTAGES OF A BOOK OF LISTS OVER MANY OTHER CATEGORIES OF PRESENTING INFORMATION

meaty / regularly brief, condensed, with padding removed

interesting / for someone who wants to know quickly, the information is compactly presented

factual / regularly, consists of facts

useful / as a rule; sometimes frothy

understandable / regularly

entertaining / often

mind-stimulating / often

laughter-provoking / often, if well chosen and well edited.

10 KINDS OF LISTS THAT CAN BE OF GREAT VALUE AND USEFULNESS

an inventory / that can tell the names of all the members of a class of things

a sequence / so that you know just how to locate a particular member

a table / so that if you know X, you can find the corresponding Y

a summary / so that you can remember the most significant concepts, terms, propositions, and relations of some subject

a mnemonic / like VIBGYOR (for "violet, indigo, blue, green, yellow, orange, red") so that you can remember the sequence of colors in the rainbow

an incantation or spell / so that if you believe in mystical existence you can invoke or summon spirits

a recipe / so that you can cook certain food

a score for music / so that if you can read the sequence of notes, chords, timing, etc., you can grasp the music

a computer program / so that you can change input data into desired output data

a series of numbers / like 1, ½, ¼, ⅛, ⅟16, ⅟32...for which the limit of the sum is 2

5 GRADES FOR MEASURING KNOWLEDGE OF A PERSON ABOUT A SUBJECT

1. If a person can say NO true statements about a subject, then he is IGNORANT of it.
2. If a person can say 4 true statements (that are independent) about a subject, then he is ACQUAINTED with it.
3. If a person can say 15 true independent

statements about a subject, then he is FAMILIAR with it.

4. If a person can say 40 true independent statements about a subject, then he is an EXPERT in it.

5. If a person can say 80 true independent statements about a subject, then he is a SCHOLAR of it.

Notes:

1. Independence: In the foregoing context, the statements are independent if none are deducible from one or more of the others. For example:

    A: The density of lead is 19 times the density of water.

    B. Lead has a gray color.

are independent statements.

2. Approximate Measurement: This measure (of the amount of knowledge of a person) estimated in this way is approximate, and is not intended to be accurate.

3. Context: There are some small subjects (branches of knowledge); for example, the six kinds of pieces in the game of chess, and their moves on the chessboard. In such a context, it is possible to know all the independent statements that can be made about that subject; and the foregoing numbers 4, 15, 40, and 80 do not apply.

4 WAYS OF DISGUISING INFORMATION

Obscurities / Use terms that are obscure or undefined, instead of terms that have been defined or are easy to understand.

Subjectivity / Base the information on subjective perceptions from imaginary worlds (such as opinions), instead of factual data from the real world.

Uselessness / Report information that can never be very useful or is almost useless, thus occupying time and space needed for absorbing useful information.

Padding / Pump up the information with a large amount of padding, instead of keeping just enough padding so that a reader is able to absorb ideas at a reasonably convenient rate.

6 DEFINITIONS OF THE WORD "ALMANAC"

A publication containing astronomical and meteorological data arranged according to the days, weeks, and months of a given year and often including a miscellany of other information.

A publication containing statistical, tabular, and other information.

A publication containing a collection of useful or otherwise interesting facts or statistics, usually in the form of tables and often covering the period of a given year.

A publication containing data and statistics on royal and titled families of Europe.

A book or table containing a calendar of the days, weeks, and months of the year, a register of ecclesiastical festivals and saints' days, a record of various astronomical phenomena, and optionally:

- prognostications and prophecies;
- astrological matter;
- wise and witty sayings (*Poor Richard's Almanac* by Benjamin Franklin);
- details concerning the administration and statistics of different states of the world; etc.

A table giving for stated times the apparent positions and other numerical data relating to the sun, planets, important stars, eclipses, and other matter useful to astronomers and navigators (*Astronomical Ephemeris* or *Nautical Almanac*).

(Source: various dictionaries and the Encyclopedia Britannica, 11th edition)

1 Computers and People

THE MOST IMPORTANT ASPECT OF COMPUTERS

One of the most important aspects of computers is people.

Without people to think of them, to plan them, to arrange to manufacture them, to think of the expression of systems of commands to make them do useful work, to look at the environment of problems, to imagine the solutions that can be incorporated in computers, computers would not exist. The only computers that have evolved naturally in the course of millions and millions of years of evolution are the computers that exist in the brains of animals. As C.P. Snow, the English scholar who was at one time minister of technology and science in a Labor government and who was the author of *The Two Cultures*, said, "The computer is by far the most remarkable machine invented by man."

38 PRESIDENTS OF THE AMERICAN SOCIETY FOR INFORMATION SCIENCE

Starting	President
1937	Watson Davis
1944	Keyes D. Metcalf
1945	Waldo G. Leland
1946	Watson Davis
1947	Waldo G. Leland
1948	Vernon D. Tate
1950	Luther H. Evans
1953	E. Eugene Miller
1954	Milton O. Lee
1955	Scott Adams
1956	Joseph Hilsenrath
1957	James W. Perry

1958	Herman H. Henkle
1959	Karl F. Heumann
1960	Cloyd Dake Gull
1961	Gerald J. Sophar
1962	Claire K. Schultz
1963	Robert M. Hayes
1964	Hans Peter Luhn
1965	Laurence B. Heilprin
1966	Harold Borko
1967	Bernard M. Fry
1968	Robert S. Taylor
1969	Joseph Becker
1970	Charles P. Bourne
1971	Pauline A. Atherton
1972	Robert J. Kyle
1973	John Sherrod
1974	Herbert S. White
1975	Dale B. Baker
1976	Melvin S. Day
1977	Margaret T. Fischer
1978	Audrey N. Grosch
1979	James M. Cretsos
1980	Herbert B. Landau
1981	Mary C. Berger
1982	Ruth L. Tighe
1983	Charles H. Davis

(Source: American Society for Information Science, 1010 16th St., NW, Washington, DC 20036)

19 PRESIDENTS OF THE ASSOCIATION FOR COMPUTING MACHINERY (ACM)

Starting	President
1947	John H. Curtiss
1948	John W. Mauchly
1950	Franz L. Alt
1952	Samuel B. Williams
1954	Alston S. Householder

1956	John W. Carr III
1958	Robert W. Hamming
1960	Harry D. Huskey
1962	Alan J. Perlis
1964	George E. Forsythe
1966	Anthony G. Oettinger
1968	Bernard A. Galler
1970	Walter M. Carlson
1972	Anthony Ralston
1974	Jean E. Sammet
1976	Herbert R. J. Grosch
1978	Daniel D. McCracken
1980	Peter J. Denning
1982	David H. Brandin

(Source: ACM, 11 West 42nd St., New York, NY 10036)

THE 9 FOUNDING MEMBERS OF THE ASSOCIATION FOR COMPUTING MACHINERY (ACM), 1947

Edward G. Andrews / Bell Telephone Laboratories, New York, NY

Edmund C. Berkeley / Prudential Insurance Co. of America, Newark, NJ

Robert V.D. Campbell / Harvard Computation Laboratory, Cambridge, MA

John H. Curtiss / National Bureau of Standards, Washington, DC

J. Presper Eckert / Moore School of Electrical Engineering, Philadelphia, PA

John W. Mauchly / Moore School of Electrical Engineering, Philadelphia, PA

John B. Russell / Columbia University, New York, NY

Paul W. Taylor / Massachusetts Institute of Technology, Cambridge, MA

Samuel B. Williams / Bell Telephone Laboratories, New York, NY

21 PRESIDENTS OF THE ASSOCIATION FOR EDUCATIONAL DATA SYSTEMS

Starting	President
1962	Robert Gates
1963	John Caffrey
1964	Don D. Bushnell
1965	C. Taylor Whittier
1966	John W. Sullivan
1967	G. Ernest Anderson
1968	John W. Hamblen
1969	Ralph Van Dusseldorp
1970	Everett Yarbrough
1971	Sylvia Charp
1972	Russell Weitz
1973	Bruce Alcorn
1974	James P. Augustine, Jr.
1975	Thomas McConnell, Jr.
1976	E. Ronald Carruth
1977	Judith Edwards-Allen
1978	Bradford Burris
1979	Donald C. Holznagel
1980	Winston C. Addis
1981	Dennis W. Spuck
1982	A. V. Majors

(Source: The Association for Educational Data Systems, 1201 16th St., NW, Washington, DC 20036)

32 PRESIDENTS OF THE DATA PROCESSING MANAGEMENT ASSOCIATION

Starting	President
1952	Robert L. Jenal
1953	Gordon C. Couch
1954	Richard L. Irwin
1955	Robert O. Cross
1956	Donald L. Gerightly
1957	Willis L. Daniel
1958	Lester E. Hill
1959	D.B. Paquin
1960	L.W. Montgomery
1961	Alfonso G. Pia
1962	Elmer F. Judge
1963	Robert S. Gilmore
1964	John K. Swearingen
1965	Daniel A. Will
1966	Billy R. Field
1967	Theodore Rich
1968	Charles L. Davis
1969	D.H. Warnke
1970	James D. Parker
1971	Edward O. Lineback
1972	Herbert B. Safford
1973	James B. Sutton
1974	Edward J. Palmer
1975	J. Ralph Leatherman
1977	Robert J. Marrigan
1978	Delbert W. Atwood
1979	George R. Eggert
1980	Robert A. Finke
1981	P. Roger Fenwick
1982	Donald E. Price
1983	J. Crawford Turner, Jr.
1984	Carroll J. Lewis

(Source: Data Processing Management Association, 505 Busse Highway, Park Ridge, IL 60068)

20 PRESIDENTS OF THE INSTITUTE OF ELECTRICAL AND ELECTRONIC ENGINEERS COMPUTER SOCIETY* (IEEE)

Starting	President
1953	Jean H. Folker
1954	H.T. Larson

1955	Jerre D. Noe
1957	Werner Bucholz
1958	Willis H. Ware
1959	R.O. Endres
1960	A.A. Cohen
1962	W.L. Anderson
1964	K.W. Uncapher
1965	R.I. Tanaka
1966	Samuel Levine
1968	L.C. Hobbs
1970	E.J. McCluskey
1972	A.S. Hoagland
1974	S.S. Yau
1976	D. Simmons
1977	M. Smith
1979	T. Feng
1981	R. Merwin
1982	O. Garcia

*formerly the Professional Group on Electronic Computers

(Source: Institute of Electrical and Electronic Engineers, Inc., P.O. Box 639, Silver Spring, MD 20901)

15 PRESIDENTS OF THE NATIONAL ASSOCIATION FOR STATE INFORMATION SYSTEMS

Starting	President
1968	Carl Vorlander
1970	Daniel B. Magraw
1971	M. Everett McCoy, Jr.
1972	John L. Gentile
1973	Verne H. Tanner, Jr.
1974	Glenn W. Goodman
1975	Jack Newcomb
1976	Harold O. Casali
1977	W. Kenneth Hull
1978	Gerald C. Schmitz

1979	Ernest E. Kovaly
1980	Dozier Johnson
1981	George Patton
1982	Jack Stanton
1983	Jim Heck

(Source: The National Association for State Information Systems, P.O. Box 11910, Lexington, KY 40758)

5 PRESIDENTS OF THE NATIONAL COMPUTER GRAPHICS ASSOCIATION, INC.

Starting	President
1979	Richard D. Schulman
1980	Caby C. Smith
1981	William L. Howard
1982	Robert T. Aangeenbrug
1983	Ellen M. Knapp

(Source: National Computer Graphics Association, 8201 Arlington Blvd., Fairfax, VA 22031-4670)

7 PRESIDENTS OF THE RECOGNITION TECHNOLOGIES USERS ASSOCIATION

Starting	President
1970	R.R. Bower
1972	O.E. Stolberg
1974	A. Blair Jensen
1976	William A. Dwyer
1979	James J. Wilson
1981	Richard F. Burns
1983	Robert R. Montgomery

(Source: Recognition Technologies Users Association, P.O. Box 2016, Manchester Center, VT 05255)

13 PRESIDENTS OF THE SOCIETY FOR COMPUTER SIMULATION

Starting	President
1963	Maughan Mason
1965	P.J. Herman
1967	James E. Wolle
1969	David R. Miller
1970	Frank C. Rieman
1972	Jon N. Magnall
1973	George A. Rahe
1974	Robert D. Brennan
1975	Paul W. Berthiaume
1976	Per A. Holst
1977	Donald C. Martin
1979	Stewart Schlesinger
1982	Walter Karplus

(Source: Society for Computer Simulation, P.O. Box 2228, La Jolla, CA 92038)

13 PRESIDENTS OF THE SOCIETY FOR INFORMATION DISPLAY

Starting	President
1962	Harold R. Luxenberg
1963	Rudolph L. Kuehn
1964	Anthony Debons
1965	James H. Redman
1966	William P. Bethke
1968	Carl Machover
1970	Phillip P. Damon
1972	Carlo P. Crocetti
1974	Robert C. Klein
1976	Erwin A. Ulbrich
1978	Bernard J. Lechner
1980	Tarricia DuPuis
1982	Gus Carroll

(Source: Society for Information Display, 654 North Sepulveda Blvd., Los Angeles, CA 90049)

8 PRESIDENTS OF THE SOCIETY OF DATA EDUCATORS

Starting	President
1960	E. Dana Gibson
1968	Merle Wood
1970	Arthur H. Pike
1972	Boyce Quigley
1974	Lloyd D. Brooks
1978	Robert P. Behling
1980	Ben M. Bauman
1982	Gerald E. Wagner

(Source: Society of Data Educators, c/o School of Business, James Madison University, Harrisonburg, VA 22807)

12 HISTORICAL FIGURES RELATED TO THE DEVELOPMENT OF COMPUTERS

anonymous (1000 BC or earlier) / the abacus, a device for computing decimally (i.e., units, tens, hundreds, thousands, ten thousands, etc.), using small stones on a slab marked in columns, or small beads on a frame arranged with parallel rods

John Napier (1550–1617) / slide rule and logarithms for analog multiplication, and "Napier's bones" for digital multiplication

Blaise Pascal (1623–1662) / numerical adding machine using gears with ten teeth and a carry tooth

G.W. von Leibniz (1646–1716) / multiplying and dividing machine for numbers using repeated addition and subtraction

Joseph Jacquard (1752–1834) /machinery for weaving intricate designs in tapestries on looms, using punched cards with holes for selection of needles bearing different threads

Charles Babbage (1792–1871) / a "Difference Engine," and an "Analytical Engine," partially constructed; perfectly conceived general purpose computer for numbers and numerical computations

Herman Hollerith (1860–1929) / designed and produced machinery for classifying, sorting, counting, and adding cards with punched holes representing instances and numbers; first used in the tabulation of the 1890 U.S. Census; holder of nearly 50 patents on uses of punched cards for data processing; founded forerunner company to IBM

Norbert Wiener (1894–1964) / instructor at Massachusetts Institute of Technology 1919-1961; published *Cybernetics,* 1948, and *The Human Use of Human Beings,* 1950; active in mathematics, philosophy of mechanistic and mathematical systems, feedback, automata, simulation of human thought processes; more than 100 publications

Howard H. Aiken (1900–1973) / head of the Harvard Computation Laboratory, Cambridge, MA, 1939-61; here one of the first automatic digital computers,

designed and engineered by Aiken and staff, called the Mark I, started operating in 1944; it was constructed with U.S. Navy and IBM (T.J. Watson) support

Wallace J. Eckert (1902–1971) / used punch card machines, 1929-33, for interpolation of astronomical data, reduction of observational data, and numerical solution of planetary equations; published *Punched Card Methods in Scientific Calculation,* 1940; director of U.S. Nautical Almanac Office, 1940-45; head of IBM's Pure Science Department, and the T.J. Watson Scientific Computing Laboratory, 1946-67

John von Neumann (1903–1957) / active in logic, quantum theory, theory of high-speed computing machines, theory of games and strategy, applied mathematics; professor at the School of Mathematics, Institute for Advanced Study, Princeton University; planner of the Institute for Advanced Study computer; author of over 500 papers

Alan M. Turing (1912–1954) / active in mathematics, computing machines, chess, cryptanalysis, code deciphering; located at the British National Physical Laboratory and elsewhere; inventor of the "Turing Machine," which expresses the mathematical notion of effective computability; originator of remarkable software

2 Computers and Associations, Users' Groups, . . .

A REMINISCENCE ON AN EARLY COMPUTER SOCIETY

In January 1947, a "Symposium on Large Scale Calculating Machines" was held at the Harvard Computation Laboratory in Cambridge, Massachusetts. The invitations were sent out by Professor Howard H. Aiken, head of the Laboratory. I attended in two roles: first, as an actuary and a member of the Methods Division of the Prudential Insurance Company of America in Newark, New Jersey, with the title (at that time) of Chief Research Consultant; and second, as one of the group of persons who had worked at the Harvard Computation Laboratory in 1945-46 on the design and construction of the Harvard Mark II Large Scale Calculator built for the Naval Proving Ground. I had contributed a "four times a decimal digit readout" circuit for the six-pole relays of the calculator (something Aiken had said could not be done; but I had a different idea for doing it.)

There were many young people at the symposium, including Dr. John W. Mauchly of the ENIAC electronic computer group at the University of Pennsylvania. Aiken was very firmly in favor of relay calculators, and much opposed to the "unreliable" vacuum tube ones. The younger people were eager to see the formation of a society of persons interested in "large-scale calculating machinery." "Oh, not another society—save us from that," was the view of many of the older people at the symposium. But during the summer of 1947, eight contemporary friends of mine and I put together a Temporary Committee for an Eastern Association for Computing Machinery, and we agitated.

In September 1947, the Temporary Committee called a meeting at Columbia University in New York, and 57 persons attended. After a lecture by T. Kite Sharpless on magnetic media for storing information, such an association was voted into existence by the persons present. Then, in December 1947, at the Army Ballistic Research Laboratory in Aberdeen, Maryland, at a meeting hosted by Dr. Franz L. Alt, the word "Eastern" was taken off the name, and the Association for Computing Machinery began, with several hundred members enrolled by the end of the meeting.

Now the ACM has over 60,000 members, and there exist more than 100 computer societies all over the world, and more than 1000 chapters of these societies.

Such is the tide of effort for people to join each other in dealing with the ideas and realities of "automatic computing machinery."

11 CONSTITUENT SOCIETIES OF AMERICAN FEDERATION OF INFORMATION PROCESSING SOCIETIES (AFIPS)

American Society for Information Science (ASIS)
1010 16th St. NW
Washington, DC 20036

American Statistical Association (ASA)
806 15th St. NW
Washington, DC 20005

Association for Computational Linguistics (ACL)
c/o Donald Walker
SRI International, EJ278
Menlo Park, CA 94025

Association for Computing Machinery (ACM)
11 West 42nd St.,
New York, NY 10036

Association for Educational Data Systems (AEDS)
1202 16th St. NW
Washington, DC 20036

Data Processing Management Association (DPMA)
505 Busse Highway
Park Ridge, IL 60068

IEEE Computer Society (IEEECS)
10662 Los Vaqueros Circle
Los Alamitos, CA 90720

Instrument Society of America (ISA)
Box 12277
Research Triangle Park, NC 27709

Society for Computer Simulation (SCS)
P.O. Box 2228
La Jolla, CA 92038

Society for Industrial & Applied Mathematics (SIAM)
117 South 17th St.
Philadelphia, PA 19103

Society for Information Display (SID)
654 North Sepulveda Boulevard
Los Angeles, CA 90049

(Source: American Federation of Information Processing Societies, 1815 N. Lynn St., #800, Arlington, VA 22209)

43 FULL MEMBERS OF THE INTERNATIONAL FEDERATION OF INFORMATION PROCESSING

Algeria
    Commissariat National á
    l'Informatique,

Route Nationale No. 5, Cinq Maisons/
El-Harrach
Algiers, Algeria

Argentina
Sociedad Argentina de Informática e
Investigación Operativa
Avda. Santa Fe 1145
1059 Buenos Aires, Argentina

Australia
Australian Computer Society Inc.,
P.O. Box N26, Grosvenor Street
Sydney, N.S.W. 2000, Australia

Austria
Austrian Computer Society,
Wollzeile 1-3
A-1010 Vienna, Austria

Belgium
FAIB-FBVI
c/o "SOGESCI" (Mme Dufour)
Rue de la Concorde 51
B-1050 Brussels, Belgium

Brazil
SUCESU-NACIONAL
Av. W-3 Norte -Q. 504
Edificio Mariana-Sala 205
70730 Brasilia-DF, Brazil

Bulgaria
Bulgarian Academy of Sciences
1 "7th November" Street
Sofia 1000, Bulgaria

Canada
Canadian Information Processing Society (CIPS)
243 College Street West, 5th Floor
Toronto, Ontario, Canada M5T 2Y1

China, People's Republic of
Chinese Institute of Electronics
P.O. Box 139
Beijing, People's Republic of China

Cuba
Instituto de Mathemática Cibernética y
Computación
Academia de Ciencias de Cuba,
Habana 2, República de Cuba

Czechoslovakia
Ústav Technickej kybernetiky SAV
Czechoslovak National Committee for
IFIP
Dúbravská cesta, 809 31 Bratislava,
C.S.S.R.

Denmark
Danish Federation for Information Processing (DANFIP)
Kronprinsensgade 14/4
1113 Copenhagen K, Denmark

Egypt
Egyptian Computer Society,
c/o Institute of Statistical Studies and
Research
5 Tharwat Street
Orman, Giza, The A.R.E.

Finland
Finnish Data Processing Assoc.
Mikonkatu 19 A 8
SF-00100 Helsinki 10, Finland

France
Association Française pour la Cyber-
nétique Economique et Technique
(AFCET)
156, Boulevard Péreire
75017 Paris, France

German Democratic Republic
Academy of Sciences of the German
Democratic Republic
c/o Prof. Dr. N.J. Lehmann
Technische Universitat Dresden,
Bereich Mathematische Kybernetik
und Rechentechnik der Sektion
Mathematik
Mommenstrasse 13
DDR-8027 Dresden, G.D.R.

Germany, Federal Republic of
Gesellschaft fur Informatik e.V. (GI)
Postfach 16 69
5300 Bonn 1, F.R.G.

Hungary
John von Neumann Society
Anker Köz 1
Budapest 1061, Hungary

9

India
Computer Society of India
Institute of Engineers Building
15 Haji Ali Park
Bombay 400 034, India
(Att. Executive Secretary)

Iraq
Planning Board/National Computer
Centre
P.O. Box 3261 Saadoon
Baghdad, Iraq

Ireland
Irish Computer Society
16 Hume Street
Dublin 2, Ireland

Israel
Information Processing Association of
Israel (IPA),
P.O. Box 13009
Jerusalem, Israel

Italy
Associazione Italiana per il Calcolo Au-
tomatico (A.I.C.A.)
c/o FAST
Piazzale Rodolfo Morandi 2
20121 Milan, Italy

Japan
Information Processing Society of Japan
Kikai Shinko Building
3-5-8 Shiba-koen, Minato-ku
Tokyo 105, Japan

Korea, Republic of
Korea Information Science Society
K.P.O. Box 1205
Seoul 100-00, Republic of Korea

Morocco
Association Marocaine pour le Dévelop-
pement de l'Electronique, de l'Infor-
matique et de l'Automatique
(AMADEIA),
c/o Lab. d'Electronique,
Faculté des Sciences
B.P. 1014, Rabat, Morocco

Netherlands
Nederlands Genootschap voor
Informatica
Paulus Potterstraat 40
1071 DB Amsterdam, The Netherlands

New Zealand
The New Zealand Computer Society,
Inc., National Office
P.O. Box 12-249
Wellington, New Zealand

Nigeria
Computer Association of Nigeria
c/o Dept. of Computer Science
University of Ife
Ille-Ife, Nigeria

Norway
Norwegian Computer Society
P.O. Box 192, Sentrum
N-Oslo 1, Norway

Poland
Polish Academy of Sciences
00-901 Warszawa
PKiN, Poland

Portugal
Associacao Portuguesa de Informática
Av. Almirante Reis 127, 1 . Esq.
Lisbon 1, Portugal

South Africa
The Computer Society of South Africa
P.O. Box 1207
Johannesburg 2000, Republic of South
Africa

Spain
Federación Espanola de Sociedades de
Informática (FESI)
Facultad de Ciencias Fisicas
Ciudad Universitaria
Madrid 3, Spain

Sweden
Swedish Society for Information
Proccessing
Box 22114
S-104 22 Stockholm, Sweden

Switzerland
  Swiss Federation of Informatics, SVI/
    FSI
  P.O. Box 373
  CH-8037 Zurich, Switzerland
Syria
  Scientific Studies and Research Centre
  P.O. Box 4470
  Damascus, Syria
Tunisia
  Centre National de l'Informatique
  Rue Belhassen Ben Chabaane
  El Omrane, Tunis, Tunisia
United Kingdom
  The British Computer Society,
  13 Mansfield Street
  London WIM OBP, U.K.
U.S.A.
  American Federation of Information
    Processing Societies (AFIPS)
  1815 North Lynn Street, Suite 800
  Arlington, VA 22209, U.S.A.
U.S.S.R.
  The Computing Centre of the U.S.S.R.
    Academy of Sciences
  Vavilova 40
  Moscow-B-333, U.S.S.R.
Yugoslavia
  ETAN Yugoslav Committee for Elec-
    tronics and Automation
  P.O. Box 356
  11001 Belgrade, Yugoslavia
South East Asia
  South East Asia Regional Computer
    Confederation (SEARCC)
  SEARCC Secretariat
  c/o National Computer Board
  5 Portsdown Road
  Singapore 0513

37 MORE COMPUTER ASSOCIATIONS AND SOCIETIES

ADAPSO (Association of Data Processing
  Service Organizations)

1300 N. 17th St.
Arlington, VA 22209
William McGowan, Chairman

AMCEE (Association for Media-Based
  Continuing Education for Engineers)
225 North Ave. NW
Atlanta, GA 30332
David Waugh, Chairman

American Management Associations
135 W. 50th St.
New York, NY 10020

American Society for Engineering
  Education
Suite 200, 11 Dupont Circle
Washington, DC 20036

American Society for Training and De-
  velopment, Inc.
Suite 305, 600 Maryland Ave. SW
Washington, DC 20024

American Society of Mechanical
  Engineers
United Engineering Center
345 E. 47th St.
New York, NY 10017

American Voice Input/Output Society
P.O. Box 11,307A
Palo Alto, CA 94306

Association for Systems Management
P.O. Box 1115
Boston, MA 02117

Association of Computer Programmers
  and Analysts
11800 Sunrise Valley Dr., Suite 808
Reston, VA 22091
R.H. Fisher, Secretary

Association of Media Producers
1101 Connecticut Ave., Suite 700
Washington, DC 20036
Toni H. Morgan, President

CBEMA (Computer and Business Equip-
  ment Manufacturers Association
Suite 500, 311 First St. NW
Washington, DC 20001
V.E. Henriques, President

11

CDLA (Computer Dealers and Lessors Association)
1212 Potomac St. NW
Georgetown, Washington, DC 20007
G. Heilborn, President

Computec (Computer Technology Division of Instrument Society of America)
67 Alexander Dr.
Research Triangle Park, NC 27709
H. Zinschlag, Director

Computer and Automated Systems Association of the Society of Manufacturing Engineers
1 SME Drive, P.O. Box 930
Dearborn, MI 48128
R.G. Abraham, President

Computer and Communications Industry Association
1500 Wilson Blvd., Suite 512
Arlington, VA 22209

Data Processing Management Association, Education Foundation
505 Busse Highway
Park Ridge, IL 60068
D. Price, President

DEMA (Data Entry Management Association
P.O. Box 3231
Stamford, CT 06905
N. Bodek, President

Electronic Funds Transfer Association
Suite 200, 1312 Eighteenth St. NW
Washington, DC 20036

Inter-Calc (formerly Visi-Group)
25 Roxbury Rd.
P.O. Box 254
Scarsdale, NY 10583

Japan Society, Inc.
333 E. 47th St.
New York, NY 10017

Japan Software Industry Association
5-8 Shibakoen, 3 Chome, Minato-ku
Tokyo, Japan
S. Shimokura, Secretary General

Mumps Users' Group
c/o Professional Associates
2012 Big Bend Blvd.
St. Louis, MO 63117

National Association of Relay Manufacturers
P.O. Box 1505
Elkhart, IN 46515
A.C. Johnson, Executive Director

National Computer Graphics Association, Inc.
2033 M Street NW, Suite 330
Washington, DC 20036
E.K. Zimmerman, Executive Director

National Micrographics Association
8719 Colesville Rd.
Silver Spring, MD 20910
C.S. Myers, Public Relations Director

NFAIS (National Federation of Abstracting & Indexing Services)
112 South 16th St.
Philadelphia, PA 19102
R.L. Wigington, President

Recognition Technologies Users Association (formerly OCR Users Association)
P.O. Box 2016
Manchester Center, VT 05255

SME (Society of Manufacturing Engineers)
One SME Drive, P.O. Box 930
Dearborn, MI 48128
J. Tlusty, President

Societe Europeenne de Mini-Informatique et de Systemes (SEMS)
Les Bureaux du Parc
36-38 Rue de la Princesse
B.P. 478430 Louveciennes, France

Societe Francaise d'Equipment pour la Navigation Aerienee
Data Processing Division
10 Bis, Rue Paul Dautier
B.P. 59
78140 Velizy, France

Society for the Advancement of Material & Process Engineering
Box 613
Azusa, CA 91702
J. Dyer, President

Society of Data Educators
School of Business Administration
James Madison University
Harrisonburg, VA 22801

Society of Photographic Scientists and Engineers
7003 Kilworth Lane
Springfield, VA 22151
R.H. Wood, Executive Director

SOLINET (Southeastern Library Network, Inc.)

Plaza Level, 400 Colony Square
1201 Peachtree St. NE
Atlanta, GA 30361
H.F. Johnson, Chairman

SPIE (International Society for Optical Engineering)
P.O. Box 10
Bellingham, WA 98227

Structured Systems Group
5204 Claremont St.
Oakland, CA 94618

World Future Society (WFS)
4916 St. Elmo Ave.
Bethesda, MD 20814
E. Cornish, President

3 Computers and Magazines

- Magazines Dealing Often with Computers

221 MAGAZINES, JOURNALS, BULLETINS, AND PERIODICALS IN THE FIELD OF COMPUTERS AND DATA PROCESSING

ABA Banking Journal
American Bankers Association
345 Hudson St.
New York, NY 10014

ACM Computing Surveys
Association for Computing Machinery
11 W. 42nd St.
New York, NY 10036

ACM Newsletter
11 W. 42nd St.
New York, NY 10036

Across the Board
845 Third Ave.
New York, NY 10022

Administrative Management
Geyer-McAllister Publications, Inc.
51 Madison Ave.
New York, NY 10010

Advanced Management Journal
135 W. 50th St.
New York, NY 10020

AEDS Bulletin, Journal and Monitor
1201 16th St., NW
Washington, DC 20036

American Academy of Actuaries Newsletter
1835 K St., NW, Suite 515
Washington, DC 20006

American Scientist
345 Whitney Ave.
New Haven, CT 06511

APL Market Newsletter
P.O. Box 5314
Mt. Carmel, CT 06518

Asian Computer Monthly
Computer Publications Ltd.
Seabird House, 7th Floor
22 Wyndham St.
Hong Kong

*Association of Computer Users Newsletter
 and Bulletin*
P.O. Box 9033
Boulder, CO 80301

Australian Computer Journal
P.O. Box N26, Grosvenor St.
Sydney, NSW 2000, Australia

Autotransaction Industry Report
International Data Corp.
5 Speen St.
Framingham, MA 01701

Bank Administration
60 Gould Ctr.
Rolling Meadows, IL 60068

Big Byte, The
Pansonic Systems Inc.
709 Enterprise Dr.
Oak Brook, IL 60521

Business Press Service
U.S. Dept. of Labor
Office of Information
Washington, DC 20210

Byte
70 Main St.
Peterborough, NH 03458

CA Magazine
Institute of Canadian Chartered
 Accountants
250 Bloor St., E
Toronto, M4W 1G5, Ontario, Canada

Canadian DataSystems
Maclean-Hunter Ltd.
481 University Ave.
Toronto, Ontario, M5W 1A7, Canada

CBEMA, Computer and Business Equipment Manufacturers Association
311 First Street, NW, Ste. 500
Washington, DC 20001

Cerberus Report, The
P.O. Box 470
Frenchtown, NJ 08825

Charles Babbage Institute Newsletter, The
University of Minnesota
104 Walter Library
117 Pleasant St., SE
Minneapolis, MN 55455

*CIME, Computers in Mechanical
 Engineering*
American Society of Mechanical
 Engineers
345 E. 47th St.
New York, NY 10017

CIPS Review
Canadian Information Processing Society
243 College St., Fifth Floor
Toronto, Ontario, M5T 2Y1, Canada

Collegiate Microcomputer
Division of Mathematics
Rose-Hulman Institute of Technology
Terre Haute, IN 47803

Columbia Journal of World Business
814 Uris Hall
Columbia University
New York, NY 10027

Communications
1615-A West Sixth St.
Austin, TX 78703

Communications
Cardiff Publishing Co.
3900 S. Wadsworth Blvd.
Denver, CO 80235

Communications of ACM
11 W. 42nd St.
New York, NY 10036

Compute
Box 5119
Greensboro, NC 27403

Computer
IEEE Service Center
445 Hoes Lane
Piscataway, NJ 08854

Computer Age
7620 Little River Turnpike
Annandale, VA 22003

Computer-Asia
Shing Lee Commercial Bldg.
19th Floor
6-12 Wing Kut St.
Hong Kong

Computer Communications
IPC Science and Technology Press, Ltd.
P.O. Box 63
Westbury House, Bury St.
Guildford, Surrey GU2 5BH, England

Computer Decisions
Hayden Publishing Co., Inc.
50 Essex St.
Rochelle Park, NJ 07662

Computer Graphics News
National Computer Graphics Assoc.
8401 Arlington Blvd., Ste. 601
Fairfax, VA 22031

Computer Law and Tax Report
100 Tower Office Park
Woburn, MA 01801

Computer/Law Journal
P.O. Box 54308 T.A.
Los Angeles, CA 90054

Computerletter
Datacrown
650 McNicoll Ave.
Willowdale, Ontario, Canada, M2H ZE1

Computer Negotiations Report
Sunscape International, Inc.
1513 E. Livingston St.
Orlando, FL 32803

Computers and Standards
North Holland Publishing Co.
P.O. Box 211
1000 AE Amsterdam, The Netherlands

Computer Security, Auditing and Controls
Management Advisory Publications
P.O. Box 151
Wellesley Hills, MA 02181

Computer Security
Computer Security Institute
43 Boston Post Road
Northborough, MA 01532

Computers in Industry
North Holland Publishing Co.
P.O. Box 103
1000 AC, Amsterdam, The Netherlands

Computers in Mechanical Engineering
345 E. 47th St.
New York, NY 10017

Computers & Medicine
American Medical Association
Box 36
Glencoe, IL 60022

Computers & Operations Research
Pergamon Press, Ltd.
Headington Hall
Oxford OX3 OBW, England

Computers and People
Berkeley Enterprises, Inc.
815 Washington St.
Newtonville, MA 02160

Computers and Security
North Holland Publishing Co.
P.O. Box 103
1000 AC Amsterdam, The Netherlands

Computerworld
P. O. Box 880
Framingham, MA 01701

Computing
VNU Business Publications BV
55 Frith St.
London W1A 2HG, England

Creative Computing
Box 789-M
Morristown, NJ 07960

Cubic Circuit
9333 Balboa Ave.
San Diego, CA 92123

Database Journal
A.P. Publications, Ltd.
322 St. John St.
London, EC1V 4QH, England

Data Comm Advisor
International Data Corp.
P.O. Box 955
Framingham, MA 01701

Data Entry Awareness Report
Management Information Corp.
140 Barclay Center
Cherry Hill, NJ 08034

Data Management
Data Processing Management Assn.
505 Busse Highway
Park Ridge, IL 60068

Data Processing
IPC Electrical-Electronic Press, Ltd.
Quadrant House, The Quadrant
Sutton, Surrey SM2 5AS England

Davis Database
111 Charlotte Place
Englewood Cliffs, NJ 07632

Decworld
129 Parker St.
Maynard, MA 01754

Digital Research News
P.O. Box 579
Pacific Grove, CA 93950

Digital Systems
Bache Halsey Stuart Shields Inc.
Bache Plaza
100 Gold St.
New York, NY 10038

*Directory of Communications
  Management*
Applied Computer Research
3003 W. Northern St., Suite 3
P.O. Box 9280
Phoenix, AZ 85068

Directory of Top Computer Executives
Applied Computer Research
3003 W. Northern St., Suite 3
P.O. Box 9280
Phoenix, AZ 85068

Dr. Dobb's Journal
Box E
Menlo Park, CA 94025

EastWest Outlook
227 Massachusetts Ave., NE, Suite 300
Washington, DC 20002

EDP Analyzer
925 Anza Ave.
Vista, CA 92083

EDPACS
Automation Training Center, Inc.
11250 Roger Bacon Dr., Suite 17
Reston, VA 22090

EDP Auditor
EDP Auditors Foundation
373 S. Schmale Road
Carol Stream, IL 60187

EDP Industry Report
P.O. Box 955
Framingham, MA 01701

EDP Performance Review
Applied Computer Research
P.O. Box 9280
Phoenix, AZ 85068

EDP Training News
Carnegie Press, Inc.
100 Kings Road
Madison, NJ 07940

EDP Japan Report
Dept. JR, International Data Corp.
5 Speen St.
Framingham, MA 01701

Electronic Mail and Message Systems
30 High St.
Norwalk, CT 06851

Elsevier Journal Information Center
52 Vanderbilt Ave.
New York, NY 10164

Ergonomics Newsletter
Koffler Group
1301 Lachman Lane
Pacific Palisades, CA 90272

Europa Report
IDC Europa Ltd.
2 Bath Road
Chiswick, 4W 1LN, London, England

Export Advisor
P.O. Box 10040
San Jose, CA 95157

Feedback from Fujitsu
Ruder Finn & Rotman Inc.
110 E. 59th St.
New York, NY 10022

Focus
Newsletter of Mathematical Association of
    America
1529 18th St. NW
Washington, DC 20036

FMS Magazine, The
Flexible Manufacturing Systems
The Press Office
IFS Publications, Ltd.
35-39 High St.
Kempston, Bedford, MK42 7BT, England

Folio
Sandra Pakin & Associates
6007 N. Sheridan Road
Chicago, IL 60660

Forbes
60 Fifth Ave.
New York, NY 10011

Fujitsu in Touch
Fujitsu Limited
Tokyo, Japan

Furrow, The
Public Relations Dept.
Deere & Co.
Moline, IL 61265

Futurist, The
World Future Society
4916 St. Elmo Ave.
Bethesda, MD 20814-5089

Government Accountants Journal
727 S. 23rd St. #120
Arlington, VA 22202

Government Executive
Executive Publications, Inc.
1725 K St., NW
Washington, DC 20006

Graphic Arts Monthly
666 Fifth Ave.
New York, NY 10103

Harfax Directory of Industry Data Sources
Ballinger Publishing Co.
54 Church St.
Cambridge, MA 02138

Harvard Business Review
Soldiers Field Station
Boston, MA 02163

High Technology & Technology Illustrated
P.O. Box 2811
Boulder, CO 80321

Hospital Newsletter
Shared Medical Systems
650 Park Ave.
King of Prussia, PA 19406

Hospital Progress
4455 Woodson Road
St. Louis, MO 63134

IBM Journal of Research and Development
IBM Corp.
Armonk, NY 10504

IBM Systems Journal
IBM Corp.
Armonk, NY 10504

IBM User, The
ECC Publications Ltd.
30-31 Islington Green
London N1, England

ICP Interface
International Computer Programs, Inc.
P.O. Box 40946
Indianapolis, IN 46240

*IEEE Computer Graphics and
  Applications*
10662 Los Vaqueros Circle
Los Alamitos, CA 90721

IEEE Micro
10662 Los Vaqueros Circle
Los Alamitos, CA 90721

IEEE Spectrum
Institute of Electrical & Electronics Engineers Inc.
345 E. 47th St.
New York, NY 10017

IMC Journal
International Micrographic Congress
P.O. Box 34404
Bethesda, MD 20817

Industrial Engineering
25 Technology Park
Atlanta, Norcross, GA 30092

Industrial Research & Development
1301 S. Grove Ave.
Barrington, IL 60010

*INFOR-Canadian Journal of Operations
  Research & Information Processing*
Journal Dept.
University of Toronto Press
5201 Dufferin St.
Downsview, Ontario, Canada M3H 5T8

*Information and Data Base Publishing
Report*
Knowledge Industry Publications Inc.
701 Westchester Ave.
White Plains, NY 10604

Information & Management
North-Holland Publishing Co.
P.O. Box 103
1000 AE Amsterdam, The Netherlands

Information and Records Management
101 Crossways Park
West Woodbury, NY 11797

Information Display
Society for Information Display
654 N. Sepulveda Blvd.
Los Angeles, CA 90049

Information Processing
IBM Corp. Information Systems Group
1133 Westchester Ave.
White Plains, NY 10604

Information Report, The
Washington Researchers
918 16th St., NW
Washington, DC 20006

*Information Retrieval & Library
Automation*
Lomond Publications, Inc.
Mt. Airy, MD 21771

Information Services & Use
North Holland Publishing Co.
P.O. Box 103
1000 AC Amsterdam, The Netherlands

Infosystems
Hitchcock Bldg.
Wheaton, IL 60187

InfoNews
Information International Inc.
5933 Slauson Ave.
Culver City, CA 90230

Information Systems Abstracts
8407 Thornberry Drive W.
Upper Marlboro, MD 20772

InfoWorld
P.O. Box 860
1200 East Street
Westwood, MA 02090

Inqwell, The
Infodata Systems Inc.
One Skyline Place
5205 Leesburg Place
Falls Church, VA 22041

Instructor
757 Third Ave.
New York, NY 10017

Instruments & Control Systems
P.O. Box 2025
Radnor, PA 19089

InTech
67 Alexander Drive
P.O. Box 12277
Research Triangle Park, NC 27709

Interactive Computing
The Association of Computer Users
P.O. Box 9003
Boulder, CO 80301

Interface Age
16704 Marquardt Ave.
Cerritos, CA 90701

Interface
ICP Inc.
P.O. Box 40946
Indianapolis, IN 46240

*International Micrographic Congress
1982-83 Source Book*
P.O. Box 34404
Bethesda, MD 20817

Interpretor
Insurance Accounting and Statistical
    Assoc.
Mutual Plaza
Durham, NC 27701

I.P. Sharp Newsletter
Box 418
Exchange Tower
2 First Canadian Pl.
Toronto, Ontario, Canada MSX 1E3

Jena Review
VE 13 Verlag Technik
Oranienburger Strasse 13/14
1020 Berlin, W. Germany

Journal of Accountancy
1211 Ave. of the Americas
New York, NY 10036

Journal of AEDS
1201 16th St., NW
Washington, DC 20036

Journal of Business
Graduate School of Business
University of Chicago Press
5801 Ellis Ave.
Chicago, IL 60637

Journal of Data Education
Official Journal of Society of Data
    Educators
School of Business Administration
James Madison University
Harrisonburg, VA 22801

Journal of Development
Box 1808
Washington, DC 20013

Journal of Documentation
3 Belgrave Sq.
London, SWI 8PL, England

Journal of Information Management
Life Office Management Association
100 Colony St.
Atlanta, GA 30361

Journal of Micrographics
8719 Colesville Rd.
Silver Spring, MD 20910

Journal of Systems Management
24587 Bagley Rd.
Cleveland, OH 44138

Jurimetrics Journal
American Bar Association
1155 E. 60th St.
Chicago, IL 60637

Kilobaud Microcomputing
Peterborough, NH 03458

Law Office Economics and Management
Callaghan & Co.
3201 Old Glenview Rd.
Wilmette, IL 60091

MACOM Newsletter
11717 Exploration Lane
Germantown, MD 20874

Management Accounting
919 Third Ave.
New York, NY 10022

Management Focus
Peat Marwick Mitchell & Co.
345 Park Ave.
New York, NY 10154

Management World
Administrative Management Society
2360 Maryland Rd.
Willow Grove, PA 19090

Manufacturing Engineering
P.O. Box 930
Dearborn, MI 48128

Micro
Box 6502
Chelmsford, MA 01824

Micrographics Newsletter
P.O. Box 313
Wykagyl Station
New Rochelle, NY 10804

*Mini-Micro Software (& Small Systems
    Software)*
A.P. Publications Ltd.
322 St. John St.
London, EC1V 4QH, England

Mini-Micro Systems
221 Columbus Ave.
Boston, MA 02116

MIS Week
Fairchild Publications
7 E. 12th St.
New York, NY 10003

Modern Materials Handling
221 Columbus Ave.
Boston, MA 02116

Monitor
Association for Media-Based Continuing
    Education for Engineeers, Inc.
225 North Ave., NW
Atlanta, GA 30332

National Report: Computers and Health
5010-1 Nicholson Lane
Rockville, MD 20852

Naval Research Reviews
Office of Naval Research
Arlington, VA 22217

Nibble
Micro-Sparc Publishing
Box 325
Lincoln, MA 01773

North Star Notes
North Star Computers, Inc.
14440 Catalina St.
San Leandro, CA 94577

Office Automation News
Office Automation Society International
4500 Four Mile Run Dr., Suite 334
Arlington, VA 22204

Office Technology Management
TRI Newsletter Associates
10076 Boca Entrada Blvd.
Boca Raton, FL 33433

onComputing
70 Main St.
Peterborough, NH 03458

Optimum
Bureau of Management Consulting
365 Laurier Ave. W.
Ottawa, Ont., Canada K1A 0S5

Optical Memory Newsletter
P.O. Box 14817
San Francisco, CA 94114

Paperwork Simplification
Standard Register Co.
P.O. Box 1167
Dayton, OH 45401

*PC News (Independent Guide to IBM Per-
    sonal Computers)*
1528 Irving St.
San Francisco, CA 94122

PC World
555 De Haro St.
San Francisco, CA 94107

Personal Computing
167 Corey Rd.
Brookline, MA 02146

Planning
American Planning Association
1776 Massachusetts Ave., NW
Washington, DC 20036

Police & Security Bulletin
Lomond Systems, Inc.
P.O. Box 88
Mt. Airy, MD 21771

Popular Computing
70 Main St.
Peterborough, NH 03458

Popular Lawyer, The
4025 Chestnut St.
Philadephia, PA 19104

Price-Waterhouse Review
1251 Ave. of the Americas
New York, NY 10020

Privacy Journal
P.O. Box 8844
Washington, DC 20003

Production Engineering
Penton Publishing Co.
Penton Plaza
1111 Chester Ave.
Cleveland, OH 44114

Quality Management Monthly
Software Research Association
P.O. Box 2432
San Francisco, CA 94126

Quick Strokes
Box 643
W. Sacramento, CA 95691

Real Times
Modular Computer Systems, Inc.
1650 W. McNab Rd.
Ft. Lauderdale, FL 33310

Recreational Computing
1263 El Camino Real
Box E
Menlo Park, CA 94025

Recreational Programmer
P.O. Box 2571
Kalamazoo, MI 49003

Retail Control
National Retail Merchants Association
100 W. 31st St.
New York, NY 10017

Sandia Science News
Box 5800
Albuquerque, NM 87185

Savings and Loan News
111 E. Wacker Dr.
Chicago, IL 60601

Savings Bank Journal
200 Park Ave.
New York, NY 10017

Scientific American
415 Madison Ave.
New York, NY 10017

S-Eighty
Milford, NH 03005

Silicon Gulch Gazette
Computer Faire
345 Swett Rd.
Woodside, CA 94062

Simulation
The Society for Computer Simulation
P.O. Box 2228
La Jolla, CA 92038

Sloan Management Review
Sloan School of Management
M.I.T.
55 Memorial Dr.
Cambridge, MA 02139

Small Business Computer News
Management Information Corp.
140 Barclay Center
Cherry Hill, NJ 08034

Small Systems Software & Mini Micro
Software
A.P. Publications Ltd.
322 St. John St.
London, EC1V 4QH, England

Small Systems World
950 Lee St.
Des Plaines, IL 60016

SoftSide
Milford, NH 03055

Softalk
10432 Burbank Blvd.
North Hollywood, CA 91601

Software
Rational Data Systems
205 E. 42nd St.
New York, NY 10017

Software News
5 Kane Industrial Dr.
Hudson, MA 01749

Software Practice and Experience
John Wiley & Sons, Ltd.
Baffins Lane
Chichester, Sussex, England

Software World
A.P. Publications Ltd.
322 St. John St.
London, EC1V 4QH, England

Solinews
Solinet Newsletter
1201 Peachtree St, NE
Atlanta, GA 30361

Solutions
Intel Corp.
3065 Bowers Ave.
Santa Clara, CA 95051

Sources
Applied Computer Research
3003 W. Northern, Suite 3
Phoenix, AZ 85068

System Development
Applied Computer Research
3003 W. Northern, Suite 3
Phoenix, AZ 85068

Systems, Objectives, Solutions
North Holland Publishing Co.
P.O. Box 103
1000 AC Amsterdam, The Netherlands

Systems User
60 S. Main St.
Janesville, WI 53545

TCS Software
TCS Dealers Association
3209 Fondren Rd.
Houston, TX 77063

Technology Review
77 Massachusetts Ave., Bldg. 10, Room 140
Cambridge, MA 02139

Technology Today
Ontario Research Foundation
Sheridan Park Research Community
Mississauga, Ont., Canada L5K 1B3

T.H.E. Journal
Information Synergy, Inc.
P.O. Box 992
Acton, MA 01720

Today's Executive
Price-Waterhouse Management Advisory
  Services
1251 Ave. of the Americas
New York, NY 10020

U F Engineering
College of Engineering
Univ. of Florida
Gainesville, FL 32611

User's Guide, The
P.O. Box 3050
Stanford, CA 94305

Vectors
Hughes Aircraft Company
Bldg. 100, M/S C-680
P.O. Box 90515
Los Angeles, CA 90009

Videoprint
30 High St.
Norwalk, CT 06851

Watnews
Computer Systems Group
University of Waterloo
Waterloo, Ont., Canada N2L 3G1

Western Electric Engineer
222 Broadway
New York, NY 10038

What's Happening in Electronics
Fujitsu Ltd.
Rosei Bldg. 4-2
Higashi Azabu 1 Chome, Minato-Ku
Tokyo 106, Japan

Which Computer?
30-31 Islington Green
London, N1 8BJ, England

Which Word Processor?
30-31 Islington Green
London, N1 8BJ, England

Word Processing & Information Systems
Geyer-McAllister Publishing, Inc.
51 Madison Ave.
New York, NY 10010

World-Wide Communications Journal
GTE Automatic Electric
400 N. Wolf Rd.
Northlake, IL 60164

W P News
Word of Mouth Enterprises
1765 N. Highland, #306
Hollywood, CA 90028

Yourdon Report, The
Yourdon, Inc.
1133 Ave. of the Americas, Suite 3830
New York, NY 10036

Xerox Exchange
Xerox Learning Systems
1600 Summer St.
Stamford, CT 06904

4 Computers and Topics

- An Approach to System, Order, and Computers
- Computing Concepts of Maximum Importance
- Key Ideas for Explaining Computers to Everybody
- Classifications of Computer Subjects
- Subject Areas of the Examination for the Certificate of Data Processing
- Topics in "BASIC: A Computer Language for Managers"
- Topics in Office Automation

AN APPROACH TO SYSTEM, ORDER, AND COMPUTERS

When I was at college preparatory school in the years 1923 to 1925, at Exeter, NH, I found out from a chemistry course I was taking and from a book I read, called *The New Knowledge*, that the periodic table of chemical elements indicated that there were exactly 92 elements. In other words, all the stuff of the physical world was composed not of fire, earth, air, and water, but of the 92 chemical elements and nothing beyond that. How exciting! So if I could remember these elements, like carbon, silicon, gold, calcium, hydrogen, and so on, I would know entirely how the whole world was made. That was intellectual honey!

So, I promptly decided to learn by heart the list of chemical elements, and did. I memorized the entire list of those that had been found and named. Unfortunately, I memorized them in alphabetical order (not in order of atomic number—that concept was just beginning): "Actinium, Aluminum, Antimony, Argon, Arsenic, Barium, Beryllium, Bismuth, Boron, Bromine," all the way down to "Zinc, Zirconium." There were three delicious th's in the T section, "Thallium, Thorium, Thulium." I can still rattle off that out-of-date 1925 list as if it were the alphabet.

It was a pleasant idea, and very satisfying to me for many years, until quite inconveniently the transuranium elements began to be made, and new elements like masurium and rhenium were named. Also, isotopes were discovered. And so, as usual in this real world, some neat and simple ideas and theories became modified and disturbed because the real world is more complicated than the ideas.

I found the same satisfying completeness of a system of ideas (or a good approximation to it) in many parts of mathematics, like the algebra of groups and Boolean algebra. Mathematics became my favorite subject of study. In the 1930's I started to learn about computers and their ramifications. That was more exciting still, for they promised to make "all the language of thought become calculable like mathematics" —still more intellectual jam.

The topics in detailed outlines of courses in the computer field for updating the training of computer people are useful, detailed maps of the "elements" and organization of many smaller subdivisions of computer science. In this way we can create an atlas, a thesaurus, a treasury, of words and ideas for each of the fields and pastures of computer science.

28 COMPUTING CONCEPTS OF MAXIMUM IMPORTANCE

algorithm / an effective calculating procedure

character / a mark or sign that may have meaning or may convey meaning

computer / a machine that carries out a flexible sequence of reasonable operations upon information

computing / carrying on a definite reasoning process with pieces of information; calculating

CPU / central processing unit; essentially a factory for producing new information out of prior information

data / given information; also calculated information

debugging / removing errors from a computer program

idea / a concept; a meaning; the meaning which is common to a set of marks all of which have the same meaning

information / marks that have meaning; a string of characters that has meaning

input / entering information into a computer in computer readable form

instruction / command; order; statement of a step in a reasoning process

language / a systematic way of representing meaning with marks, characters, or symbols

memory / places or locations in which information is stored

notation / a scheme for representing numbers or other information for computing purposes or linguistic purposes

operation / a way of combining information to produce new information

output / putting information out of a computer into human readable form

peripherals / a set of data processing equipment which surrounds a central processing unit and which gives it information or takes information from it

procedure / a sequence of steps or instructions

processing / handling a sequence of operations upon information

program / a sequence of instructions for execution by a computer

reasoning / operating logically, arithmetically, or sensibly upon information

string / a linear set of characters

system / a collection of operations and procedures organized together to accomplish a specific purpose

systems analysis / the process of recognizing a set of procedures in a human activity and specifying them in such fashion that a computer programmer can express the procedures adequately in a computing system

time-sharing / automatic apportionment of small intervals of time by a computer system so as to service a number of concurrent users without apparent delay

translating / changing from one language to another so that meaning is preserved

variable / a common noun which has one or more proper nouns to exemplify it; also the name of a class of entities, each of which is called a value of the variable; examples: address, sex, location, date, stock number, quantity on order, customer, credit, shipper, supplier, expense, reorder point, etc.; also called heading, item, data name, parameter, etc.

word / a string of marks or characters set off from other strings by spaces or other punctuation

Linguistic Concepts:
  symbol
  ideograph
  character (alphabetical, digital, punctuation, ...)
  string
  number
  information
  word (phrase, statement, paragraph, ...)
  language (semantics, syntax, grammar)
  translating

Mathematical and Logical Concepts:
  idea
  variable (pronoun, heading, ...)
  values
  reasoning (arithmetical, logical)
  operation
  command (instruction, order)
  data
  computing
  formulas (rules, graphs, functions, tables)
  algorithm
  problem (solution, answer)

System Concepts:
  system (system analysis)
  processing (programs, procedures)
  debugging
  feedback (prediction, estimating)
  organism (robot)
  establishment

35 KEY IDEAS FOR EXPLAINING COMPUTERS TO EVERYBODY

Hardware Concepts:
  computer
  input
  output
  memory (storage)
  central processing unit (arithmetical and control unit)
  bus
  peripherals
  time-sharing
  brains

28 REASONABLE CLASSIFICATIONS OF THE SUBJECTS INCLUDED UNDER COMPUTERS AND DATA PROCESSING

Administration of Computer Centers
Applications of Computers
Artificial Intelligence
Computer Circuits
Computer Components
Computer Systems
Data Bases

Decision Tables
Design and Construction of Computers
Evaluation of Software
Graphics
Information Retrieval
Information Theory
Legislation Regarding Computers
Logical Design
Management Data Processing
Mathematics of Computation
Philosophical Implications of Computers
Professional Implications from Computers
Programming Languages
Real-Time Systems
Simulation and Modeling
Social Implications of Computers
Software
Supervisory Systems for Computers
Switching Theory
Symbolic Algebraic Manipulation by
  Computers
Utility Programs

74 SUBJECT AREAS OF THE EXAMINATION FOR THE CERTIFICATE IN DATA PROCESSING

Data Processing Equipment
  Computers
    Evolution of Data Processing
    Computer Components and Functions
    Internal Processing
    Computer Characteristics
  Peripheral Equipment
    Input/Output Media
    Data Transmission
    Special Hardware
    Auxiliary Memory
Computer Programming and Software
  Principles of Programming
    Basic Computer Instruction
    Methods of Addressing
    Loops
    Subroutines
    Program Checking
    Basic Programming Techniques

Input/Output Considerations
    Advanced Programming Techniques
  Meta Programming Systems
    Assemblers
    Compilers
    Translators
    Interpreters
    Generators
    Operating Systems
    Utilities
    Data Base Management Systems
  Programming Languages
    Application, Scope and Usage
    COBOL

Principles of Management
  Principles of General Management
    Functions of Management
    Organization Principles
    General Management Techniques
    The Art of General Management
    Legal Considerations
  Data Processing Management
    General
    Systems and Programming
      Management
    Installation/Operations Management
    Security

Quantitative Methods
  Accounting and Financing
    The Basic Accounting Process
    Cost Accounting
    Internal Control
    Auditing EDP Systems
    Use of Financial Information
  Mathematics
    Mathematical Notation
    Computation Topics
    Operations Research (OR)
    Sequences
    Counting or Enumeration
    Relations, Functions, and Graphs
    Mathematics of Finance and
      Accounting
  Statistics
    Basic Statistics
    Probability Theory
    Time Series Analysis
    Control Charts

Systems Analysis and Design
  Defining the System Responsibility
    Management and User Roles
    Concepts
    Planning
    Team Organization
    Control
  Data Processing Systems Analysis
    The Feasibility Study
    Systems Investigation
    Equipment Considerations
  Data Processing Systems Design
    The Systems Approach
    File Design and Organization
    System Input
    Output in Data Processing Systems
    Other Activities
  Implementing the System
    Project Planning and Control
    Scheduling the Installation Phase
    Planning the Conversion
    Formulating the Test Cases
    Special Control and Audit Considerations during the Cut-Over Period
    Interim Procedures
    Measuring System Performance Against Specifications
  System Maintenance and Follow-Up
    Post-Installation Changes
    Periodic Reviews of System Performance
    Collecting and Analyzing Operating Costs

18 TOPICS OF A COURSE "BASIC: A COMPUTER LANGUAGE FOR MANAGERS"

Computing as a Management Tool
Executive Computing
  Problem Solving
  Planning
  Forecasting
  Database systems
Programming Fundamentals
  The mindless computer

Sequence, decision, and iteration
Computer languages
BASIC

Simple Examples
  Profit and loss
  Compound interest
  Return on investment
  Discounted cash flow

Problem solving
  Trial and error
  Structured analysis and design

Simulation and Modeling
  Probability
  Random processes
  Monte Carlo simulation

26 TOPICS IN OFFICE AUTOMATION

Automated Office Services
Automated Typewriters
Business Computer Systems
Business Systems Software
Copiers
Dictation Equipment
Display Terminals
Graphics
Interfaces
Labeling Systems
Management Control Systems
Memory Filing Systems
Memory Supplies
Microfilm Systems
Optical Readers
Paper Feed Systems
Photocomposition Equipment
Printed Computer Forms
Printers
Specialized Furniture
Telecommunications Equipment
Telephone Facsimile Equipment
Text Entry and Editing Equipment
Training Services
Voice Communication Systems
Word Processors

5 Computers and Applications, Uses, Occupations, . . .

TWO HISTORICAL APPLICATIONS

The first two historical applications of operating computers (or as they were then called "automatic large-scale calculating machines") in the United States were military. These were:

1. the Electronic Numerical Integrator and Calculator (ENIAC) at the Moore School of Electrical Engineering, Philadelphia, Pennsylvania, devoted to computing trajectory tables for the Army. ENIAC started in 1945.

2. the Harvard IBM Automatic Sequence-Controlled Calculator (Mark I) at the Harvard Computation Laboratory, Cambridge, Massachusetts, was devoted most of the time to computing trajectory tables for the Navy. When it was not needed for that purpose, it was devoted to computing tabulated values of Bessel functions, so that the crew at the laboratory (I was there) often called her "Bessie the Bessel Engine." Mark I started in 1944.

Professor Howard H. Aiken, head of the Harvard Computation Laboratory, believed that the trajectory calculations would be ephemeral, useful for only a year or two, but that the volumes of the values of Bessel functions would remain a lasting monument to a pioneer computer for decades.

But history has a way of superseding most monuments rather quickly. The tables of Bessel functions, like almost all the tables of the 1940's and earlier, have become obsolete, because a modern fast computer using rapid approximation formulas can nearly always calculate a good value of a desired mathematical function in much less time than anybody can look it up in a table.

Thus pass the expectations and monuments of man.

109 APPLICATIONS OF COMPUTERS IN OPERATIONS OF AN OFFICE

Absenteeism reports

Accounts receivable: posting, rebilling

Advertising effectiveness: analysis, data handling, etc.

Attendance records: analysis, evaluation

Billing and invoicing

Budgeting

Capital investments: analysis, evaluation

Catalog indexing

Charitable contributions: recording, analysis

Consumer credit: recording, verification

Contracts: lists, categories, analysis

Correspondence: personalized letters for solicitation, for delinquent accounts, etc.

Cost accounting: analysis, evaluation

Data gathering from multiple locations

Depreciation calculations, records

Dispatching

Energy use: analysis, reports, automatic control

Equipment: registers, transactions

Expenses: analysis, reports

File maintenance

Filing operations: single, multiple

Financial statements

Fixed assets accounting

Forecasting

General ledger: operations

Hiring: analysis

Information retrieval

Insurance: records, schedules

Inventory control

Job placement: matching people with jobs

Labor cost determinations

Lease and rental accounting

Libraries: classification, records, holdings

Linear programming

Mailing list operations: addressing mail, bundling by address groupings, personalized computer letters, updating and maintaining, zip coding

Management: management games, management information systems, reports using the exception principle, simulations, statistical analysis, strategy analysis

Manhour records and analysis

Market research: studies

Message switching

Operations research applications

Optical character recognition applications

Orders, incoming: acknowledgment, analysis, filling, processing, shipping

Overhead cost allocation

Overtime reports

Parcel mailing (high volume): computerized packing, computer operated postage meter, computer operated weighing

Payroll: computation, general increases, payment, overtime reports

Pensions: reporting, updating, valuing

Personnel: planning, placement, records

PERT charts: automatic drawing, updating

Performance evaluation

Plastic plates: embossing, code-punching

Point-of-sale transactions: orders, invoices

Price analysis
Production forecasting
Property accounting
Purchase orders: issuing, followup

Questionnaire responses: analysis, summaries

Record retention and destruction: studies, schedules
Repair and maintenance: control, records, scheduling
Rent analysis
Retirement funds: records, valuation, payments

Salary advances: control
Sales: analysis, area distribution, forecasting, quota calculations
Sales order processing: customer credit checking, inventory checking, invoicing, picking-document preparation, shipping instructions
Savings bonds: deductions, deliveries
Security systems: reports, analysis, alarms
Seniority records
Social Security records
Systems: analysis, evaluation, synthesis

Taxes: calculations
Telephone calls: reporting, analysis
Transportation optimization
Traveling salesmen: scheduling
Turnover analysis

Vacations: scheduling, verifying

Wages and salaries: analysis, records, tax computations

83 APPLICATIONS OF COMPUTERS IN PLANT MANAGEMENT AND PRODUCTION

Assembly line balancing

Cartons: automatic manufacture and packaging
Construction accounting
Construction job scheduling

Conveyor systems: designing
Critical path scheduling

Delivery scheduling
Design, computer-assisted
Dispatching control

Equipment capabilities: inventory, analysis

Factory operation simulation
Fuel consumption: records, analysis

Industrial accidents: analysis
Inspection:
    planning
    scheduling
Inventory:
    control
    record maintenance

Job standards: determination

Labor management:
    remote terminal payroll system
    scheduling
Labor utilization: analysis
Lathe operations: automatic control

Machine loading schedules
Machine tools:
    control for automatic reproduction of
        complete parts
    numerical control
Machine utilization:
    analysis
    job allocation
Maintenance:
    analysis
    records
    scheduling
Manpower utilization:
    analysis
    schedules
Manufacturing, computer-assisted
Materials and parts:
    allocations
    control
    requirements
    scheduling

Order entry
Operational Planning

Optimum ordering: determination

Parts catalogs:
 changes
 construction
 control
Parts design: evaluate modifications
Parts replacement service:
 control
 scheduling
Power used:
 analysis
 reports
Precision artwork
Precision measuring
Procurement
Products:
 designing
 grading
 marketing
 profit analysis
 testing
Production:
 forecasts
 information analysis
 scheduling
 test control
Production operations: determination
 of optimum order

Quality control

Repairs:
 analysis
 control
 records
 scheduling
Route accounting (bakeries, bottling
 plants, dairies, etc.)
Routing cable and electrical wiring

Salvage records
Scrap reporting
Security system: palm identification
Shipping control
Shop scheduling, optimum
Shrinkage calculations

Traffic control
Truck maintenance

Warehouse automation
Work standards: coding analysis

101 APPLICATIONS OF COMPUTERS TO THE HUMANITIES

Anthropology
 Cords and string: analysis
 Content analysis for cross-cultural
  value study
Archeology
 American Indians prehistoric culture:
  analysis and cataloguing
 Archeological data: information re-
  trieval and analysis
 Artifacts found at sites: analysis, classi-
  fication, reconstructing
 Museum accession records: information
  retrieval and analysis
 Pottery, Egyptian: cataloguing, classifi-
  cation, storage and retrieval
 Pottery shards found at sites: analysis,
  classification, storage and retrieval
 Stones found at sites: determination
  whether of natural or human origin
  based on analysis of angles and other
  characteristics
Art
 Designs by computer
 Graphic representation by computer
 Paintings by computer: inks, oils, water
  colors
 Pictures by computer
 Sculpture: mass production
 Sèvres porcelain: cataloguing, classifi-
  cation, forgery detection
 3-D art, generation of
Games of Skill
 Bridge, bidding: championship play
 Checkers: championship play
 Chess: excellent play
 Gomoku: excellent play
 Instant Insanity: excellent play
 Kalah: excellent play
 Nim: perfect play

Quad: excellent play
Tit-tat-toe: perfect play

Genealogy
Cataloguing
Data analysis
Research
Surnames: storage and retrieval

Geography
Map production
Maps: three-dimensional
Record matching
Spatial pattern analysis
Theory testing

History
Census records—ecological implications: analysis, summaries
Congressional voting records—social implications: analysis, summaries
Court records and decisions—implications: analysis, summaries
Diplomatic records—implication re prevailing attitudes: analysis, summaries
Election statistics—implications: analysis, summaries
Research, historical: American Revolution: Massachusetts legislature, 1774-1776, analysis
Ship sailing records—historical and economic implications: analysis, summaries

Language
Ambiguity determinations
Dead languages: deciphering, translating
Human voice: analysis, simulation
Language analysis
Navajo dictionary: compilation
Navajo language: analysis
Syntax pattern analysis
Translation from one language to another
Verification of translations
Vocabulary trends: analysis
Word classification: analysis, summaries

Word frequency counts: analysis

Literature
Author determination via key function words
Author determination via style analysis
Automatic abstracting
Biblical research
Bibliography construction
Concordance construction
Index construction
Poetry style: analysis
Proofreading
"Quik-index" by keyword of titles content

Music
Composition
Composition features such as range, phrases, patterns, refrains, cadences, etc.: analysis, simulation, synthesis
Harmonies: analysis
Musical information: analysis, retrieval, storage
Music printing
Musical data bank (classical music scores): print-out in correct, music-readable form for student to practice
Organ simulation
Pitch for singers: instruction
Simulation and models
Sounds: analysis, synthesis
Statistical analysis of style
Stereophonic music: play
Thematic indexes
Typography for music research

4 OF THE MOST DESTRUCTIVE USES OF COMPUTERS

The built-in targeting of cities on the earth in missiles with nuclear warheads, which if used by anyone will produce millions of deaths, regional firestorms, vast lethal radiation,...

The registering of all persons in a nation for purposes of controlling their political attitudes and behavior

The operation of "electronic money" without methods for almost complete prevention of computer theft

The disemployment of labor without re-education and retraining of the persons displaced to perform new useful work

6 OF THE MOST CONSTRUCTIVE USES OF COMPUTERS

Finding answers to human problems by computation that could never previously be answered in any way

Performing calculations in space navigation, engine design, statistical reasoning, ..., that could never previously be performed

Enabling routine office work, routine completion of phone calls, routine check clearing, ..., in enormous quantities to be performed

Enabling productive operations in manufacturing, machining, raw material extraction, ..., to be controlled far beyond the power of human control

Producing, via satellite communication and electronic-beeping, tiny transmitters harmlessly attached to wild animals and birds, reports on their population, migration, and other activities; real-time tracking of populations

Producing, via spaceship communication, pictures and maps of Mars, Venus, and other bodies of the solar system

20 OCCUPATIONS HIGHLY SUSCEPTIBLE TO THE INROADS OF THE COMPUTER

Airplane pilot	Clerk
Astrologer	Cook
Chess player	Diagnostician

Instrument reader	Psychiatrist
Job scheduler	Researcher
Laboratory assistant	Statistician
Locomotive engineer	Stenographer
Manager	Teacher
Mathematician	Typesetter
Medical doctor	Typist

20 REMUNERATIVE OCCUPATIONS HIGHLY RESISTANT TO THE INROADS OF THE COMPUTER

Automobile repair mechanic	Newspaper reporter
Baseball professional	Plumber
Book editor	Power shovel operator
Carpenter	Racehorse jockey
Dentist	Roofer
Electrician	School bus driver
Executive vice president	Steel construction worker
Golf professional	Surgeon
Helicopter repair mechanic	Train conductor
Lawyer	Truck driver

11 EXTRAORDINARY REASONS FOR REFUSING JOB OFFERS

A computer programmer told a Houston company that she wouldn't be able to work for a 5'6" supervisor because she "couldn't respect a man" who was three inches shorter than she was.

After he had lunch with his prospective employer, a Chicago credit manager refused to accept a position with a large retail chain. The company's vice president had ordered two glasses of chablis, and the job applicant immediately decided that he didn't want to work for anyone "who obviously had a drinking problem."

An auditor turned down a job offer from a Portland firm after it refused to allow him to take his birthday and wedding anniversary as paid holidays.

A Milwaukee accountant lost a coveted position when he insisted that he couldn't report to work for a month—on his astrologer's advice.

A Denver accountant walked away when the company wouldn't allow him to keep his moped in his office "so it wouldn't be stolen."

A financial executive was about to accept a position with a San Francisco manufacturer until their personnel director told him that the company would not pay for his weekly visits to his acupuncturist.

A corporate tax manager refused a top position with an Atlanta company on the grounds that the President was some forty pounds overweight and "a man who can't take very good care of himself probably can't take very good care of his company."

An unemployed Milwaukee executive stayed unemployed when the firm refused his request for a Cadillac Seville as a company car and he rejected their offer of a Chevrolet.

A cashier lost a position with a Boston bank because the branch she would have been assigned to failed to meet her lunch-oriented requirement: it wasn't within walking distance to McDonald's.

A financial analyst said "no" to a job offer from a Los Angeles film production company because the man he would have worked for wore bow ties and he "just didn't trust" people who did.

An accountant in New York City refused to consider an excellent job across the Hudson River in New Jersey. If he were hired, he'd have to drive across the George Washington Bridge twice each day. He was sure that the bridge would collapse someday and he "just didn't want to be on it when that happened."

(*Source:* A talk before the Oregon Society of Certified Public Accountants by Robert Half, president of Robert Half Personnel Agencies, 522 Fifth Ave., New York, NY, 10036)

6 Computers and Comforting Thoughts

- Comforting Thoughts
- Comforting Thoughts for Executives Fearful of Computers
- Paraphrases of Murphy's First Law ("If Something Can Go Wrong, It Will")
- Warnings From Copier Service Man re Proper Operation of Copier Machine
- Excuses for a Closed Mind
- "Reasonable" Excuses for Failure
- Maxims of Practical Common Sense
- Laws of Bureaucracy by Thomas L. Martin, Jr.
- Laws of General Science

COMFORTING THOUGHTS

There is no doubt that a great many people look on computers with distrust, fear, and hostility. These people range from managers and executives to clerks and messengers, from senior professors of English literature to student assistants in art departments, and more.

In general, there are three methods for dealing with this kind of situation. One is advancing, tackling it. A second is retreating or retiring from it. And the third is sidestepping, avoiding the issue by one strategy or another.

Usually, people being what they are, the second and third methods involve excuses, justifications, "comforting thoughts." They are expressed inaudibly to oneself, or spoken out loud to someone else.

The great advantage of excuses is that sometimes they are true, logical, and necessary. So they have the appearance of being plausible.

The great disadvantage of excuses is that sometimes (and perhaps often) the person giving the excuse believes it. So excuses are like a self-inflicted, infectious disablement or addiction. The French have a proverb "Qui s'excuse s'accuse": he who excuses himself accuses himself.

In this chapter we begin to explore "comforting thoughts" related to computers.

12 COMFORTING THOUGHTS FOR EXECUTIVES FEARFUL OF COMPUTERS

Seminars / I should be able to find some seminars which will explain computers to me

Books / I should be able to find some books that will introduce me to computers well

Personal computer / A personal computer at home, which my family and I could experiment with and use, could teach me much

Consultants / I should be able to find friends and consultants who will guide me

Age and Status / At my age and status in the organization, I should not have to learn a burdensome amount about computers

XYZ Inc. / XYZ has such a leading position in the computer industry and such a good reputation for service that it is reasonable and safe to use my influence to award our computing contracts to them

Delegating / Although many persons say executives cannot delegate decisions about computers to staff, yet my staff should be able to advise me well

Transfer / I may be able to transfer to a position in the organization where I do not have to get involved with computers

Alliance / I should be able to make a close alliance with a good technical computer person who will work well with me for a long time

Jargon / Although the computer jargon of many data processing persons is absurd and a "snow job," yet I should be able to persuade those persons to explain simply to me

Black Box / I should be able to treat the computer department as a black box, with known inputs and known outputs, and thereby control their relationship to me

Experience / I have been in difficult situations before, and have mastered them

14 PARAPHRASES OF MURPHY'S FIRST LAW ("IF SOMETHING CAN GO WRONG, IT WILL")

There's many a slip 'twixt cup and lip.—Old Proverb

A chain is no stronger than its weakest link.—Old Proverb

If there is an opportunity to make a mistake, sooner or later the mistake will be made.—Berkeley's Second Law, 1971.

If you seek perfection, you must settle for less.

All perfection is imperfect.

True perfection is an unattainable goal.

The longer a chain, the sooner it breaks.

One should be tolerant of good approximations.

Every system has bugs; the larger the system, the more numerous the bugs.

Failure is statistically inevitable; success is statistically impossible.

Success is a rare and happy accident; failure happens nearly all the time.

If there is a 99 percent chance that each of 100 steps will go right, then the chance of all 100 going right is only 1 in 3.

If there is a 99.9 percent chance that each of 1000 steps will go right, then the chance of all 1000 going right is only 1 in 3.

If there is a 99.99 percent chance that each of 10,000 steps will go right, then the chance of all 10,000 going right is only 1 in 3.

8 WARNINGS FROM COPIER SERVICE MAN RE PROPER OPERATION OF COPIER MACHINE

This machine is subject to breakdowns during periods of critical need.

A special circuit in the machine called a "Crisis Detector" senses operator's emotional state, determining degree of desperateness to make copies.

The "Crisis Detector" then creates a malfunction proportional to the desperation of the operator.

Threatening the machine with violence increases the degree of desperateness and the degree of malfunction.

Attempts to use any other duplicating machine may cause it to malfunction also: they both belong to the same union.

It is desirable to keep cool.

It is desirable to say sweet things to the machine.

Nothing else seems to work, except carefully following the instructions in the manual, then telephoning copier service, then begging for help.

70 EXCUSES FOR A CLOSED MIND

Inertia:
   We've always done it this way.
   We did all right without it.
   Why change it? It's still working OK.
   It's too much trouble to change.

Ridicule and Scorn:
   You're two years ahead of your time.
   Can't teach an old dog new tricks.
   Where did you dig that one up?
   Not that again.
   Let's get back to reality.
   That's what we can expect from staff.
   That's too ivory tower.
   We'll be a laughing stock.

Not Me:
   That's not my job.
   That's not our problem.
   I don't like the idea.
   You're right, but...
   That's not my responsibility — I'm still in training.

Failure to Understand:
   I don't see the connection.
   What you are really saying is...

I wouldn't know how to implement that.

Impractical:
   It costs too much.
   We're all too busy to do that.
   It's too radical a change.
   That will make other equipment obsolete.
   Our organization is too small for it.
   Not practical for the people here.
   Good thought, but impractical.

No Precedent:
   It's never been tried before.
   We've never done it before.
   Has anyone else ever tried it?
   What do they do in our competitor's organization?

It's Been Tried Before (and It Did Not Work):
   We tried that before.
   I know a fellow who tried it.

Differences:
   Our place is different.
   It won't work in our organization.
   Maybe that will work in your department — but not in mine.

Non-Acceptance:
   The men will never buy it.
   The union will scream.
   Patients won't like it.
   The Executive Committee will never go for it.
   Top management would never go for it.

Delay:
   Let's shelve it for the time being.
   Let's hold it in abeyance.
   Let's give it more thought.
   Let's put it in writing.
   Let's form a committee.
   Let's all sleep on it.
   Let's make a market research test of it first.
   Don't you think we should look into it further before we act?
   This isn't the right time to make that change.

Missing Factors:
We don't have the time.
We don't have the room.
We don't have the money.
It isn't in the budget.
We don't have the equipment.
We don't have the authority.
We don't have the personnel.
Not enough help.
We're not ready for it.
It's against company policy.
That's beyond our responsibility.

Predictions:
It's impossible.
It can't work.
It won't work.
It won't pay for itself.
We'd lose money in the long run.
It will run up our overhead.
It's too simple.
It's too complicated.
People won't behave that way.
It will take too long.

93 "REASONABLE" EXCUSES FOR FAILURE

Lack of Time:
I didn't have time.
I didn't get around to doing that.
I had too much to do.
I was too busy.
There was not enough time.

Lack of Resources:
I was stymied.
I did not know what to do about that.
I forgot.
I lost the whole job somewhere.
I couldn't see my way around the obstacles.
I couldn't make up my mind.
There wasn't anything I could do about it.
I didn't notice that.
Oh, I didn't think of that.

Lack of Clear Instructions:
I didn't understand.
I couldn't guess what you wanted me to do.
I wasn't told to do that.
The instructions were poor.
I misread the instruction.
That isn't what I thought you meant.
I could not make out whether that was a big S or a little s.

Reliance on Weak Reeds:
I overslept.
I have no alarm clock.
I missed the bus.
The repairman never came.
I believed his promise, and it was no good.
Gee, I was watching that other guy, and I never saw the accident happen.
The machine you wanted me to use — well, it didn't work.

Low Standards of Work:
I thought what I did was good enough.
I couldn't do it the way you asked.
It is beyond me how to do that well.
I thought I was careful enough.

Indifference:
I could care less.
Life's too short to worry about that.
That's no skin off my back.
That's his funeral, not mine.
Who cares about that?
It won't make any difference a hundred years from now.
I don't want to be involved.
What the hell — who cares?
It doesn't really matter, you know.

Passing the Buck:
That's not my department.
That's his job not mine.
I wasn't hired to do that.
No one told me to go ahead.
I didn't think that was important.
I didn't think you would care.
I didn't know you were in a hurry for it.
How did I know that this was different?

Wait till the boss comes back and ask him.

Sick (Lack of Health):
I got nervous.
I couldn't concentrate.
I had a headache.
I had indigestion last night.
Examinations always upset me.

Lazy (Lack of Industry):
I thought it was good enough.
He said you knew him — I didn't ask the rest of his name.
He said he would call back — I didn't ask his number.
I didn't ask his address.
There was too much work — I could never have done it all.
It was too hard.

Fearful (Lack of Courage):
Why should I stick my neck out?
Who am I to disagree with him?
I thought something would go wrong.
I didn't want to get into any trouble.
Frankly, I was afraid.

Closed Mind (Lack of Willingness to Learn):
You're insulting me.
I know all about it already.
OK, OK, so I wasn't careful enough — so what?
I am not going to take that kind of guff from anybody.
I reject your criticism.
That is my own affair, and you have no business butting in.

Fake Regret:
Sorry 'bout that.
That's just too bad, isn't it?
No use crying over spilt milk.
I didn't know it was loaded.

Joy in Mistakes:
I always make mistakes — nobody's perfect.
What a boo-boo! Isn't that funny?
I thought they had given me the right suitcase, but I got the wrong one.

See that 36 — well, I just copied it once more in the wrong place.
Gee, isn't that a funny mistake!

Joy in Failure:
You can't do everything right — it's impossible.
It isn't my fault.
It can't be done; so why try?
I'm no miracle worker.
I'm no genius.
I'm no angel.
Do as I say, not as I do.
I can't do everything; there is no sense in trying.
I just don't want to work that hard; it isn't that important to me.
I'm always a loser, any way you slice it.
I'm always a failure. Ha! Ha!

10 MAXIMS OF PRACTICAL COMMON SENSE

You will always find something in the last place you look.

In order to receive a loan from a lender, you must first prove you do not need it.

Almost anything you try to fix will take longer and cost more than you think.

A prolonged "er...er...er" may give a wise man time to think, but it will give a fool something to do with his mouth.

Everyone has a scheme for getting rich, and there is a 1000 to 1 bet that it won't work.

Friends come and go but enemies remember, and that is why politicians smile and shake hands with everybody.

Often, a short cut is the longest distance between two points.

The race is not always to the swift nor the battle to the strong, but that is a good way to bet.

It is a good rule that the light at the end of the tunnel is the headlight of an oncoming train.

If you try to please everybody, you will please nobody.

(Source: Chapter 3, "Status Quo Vadis," in *Malice in Blunderland*, by Thomas L. Martin, Jr., publ. by McGraw Hill Book Co., New York, NY, 1973, 143 pp)

10 LAWS OF BUREAUCRACY BY THOMAS L. MARTIN, JR.

Executives in the hierarchies of government, education, business, industry, labor call themselves administrators, managers, leaders.

All hierarchies are occupied by two types of bureaucrats, the Abominable No Man, who always says no, and the Willingman, who tries to solve the problems.

The No Man maintains the status quo, plays diplomat, rejects conflict, avoids decisions, wants differences settled, wants extremes adjusted, seeks a "best" way.

Whoever refuses to be adjusted is a "deviant" and needs to be "treated and cured."

The Willingman directs, manages, and controls change, makes progress happen.

If you want to get along, go along.— Rayburn's rule (Sam Rayburn, former Speaker of the House of Representatives)

If you can't convince them, confuse them. —Truman's Rule (former President of the U.S.)

When it is not necessary to make a decision, it is necessary not to make a decision. —Lord Falkland's Rule

If you can avoid a decision, do so. — Dr. Sharu S. Rangnekar's 1st Rule

Things go most smoothly when the status quo is maintained, when change is slow, cautious, evolutionary.

24 LAWS OF GENERAL SCIENCE

The graveyards are full of indispensable men.

One and one does not necessarily make 11.

Logic is a systematic method for coming to the wrong conclusion with confidence.

Anything is possible but nothing is easy.

No executive ever devotes any effort to proving himself wrong.

Common sense is the least common of all senses.

A kind heart is of little value in chess.

There is always free cheese in a mousetrap.

The solution to a problem changes the nature of the problem.

Almost everything in life is easier to get into than get out of.

Half of life's experiences are below average in satisfaction.

What the large print giveth, the small print taketh away.

When eating an elephant, eat one bite at a time. —Gen. Creighton W. Abrams.

Anybody can win — unless there happens to be a second entry. —George Ade.

When all else fails, read the instructions.

An order that can be misunderstood will be misunderstood. —Army axiom.

The more ridiculous a system of beliefs, the higher the probability of its success.

The world is more complicated than most of our theories make it out to be.

Most problems have either many answers or no answers; only a few problems have a single answer.

If there is an opportunity to make a mistake, sooner or later the mistake will be made.

If you think education is expensive, try ignorance. —Derek Bok.

When in doubt, mumble. When in trouble, delegate. When in charge, ponder.

In any household junk accumulates to fill the space available for storage.

When working towards the solution of a problem, it always helps if you know the answer — provided there is a problem.

7 Computers and Reasonable Cautions

COMPUTERS AND REASONABLE CAUTIONS

The purpose of a computer in a computer installation is to produce good answers to difficult questions. But every computer in a computer installation is itself contained in a computer system that is made up of many parts: machines, people, library, supplies, energy, office space, routines, askers of problems — paying and nonpaying, consumers of solutions — paying and nonpaying, and so on.

It makes sense to think about the following: all that has to go into the computer system; how all of it will be handled; all that has to come out of the computer system.

A computer system involves people as well as computers. So it has to be managed by a manager who, if possible, is good at managing.

But also the computer system is inside a complex, larger environment. This environment has to give the computer system money, space, energy, homes, and transportation for all its workers, and so on. So the computer system has to earn its keep, by producing for the outside environment what it wants — and what it is willing to pay for.

The number of principles that the manager has to understand and apply day after day, in order to make a success of the computer installation, is probably more than a thousand, and may be more than five thousand. The installation's computer can provide help in the task of managing the computer installation — but nevertheless there are many REASONABLE CAUTIONS that the manager and his allies on the staff of the computer installation can and should exercise. In this chapter we give some lists of reasonable cautions, with regard to many aspects, including explaining to people, the analog of explaining to a computer.

20 QUESTIONS FOR CHECKING WORK AND FIGURES

Substance:

Is the SUBSTANCE accurate? or appropriately accurate?

Is it complete? or sufficiently complete?

Has anything been left out which should be put in?

Has anything been put in which should be left out?

Does it make sense? Is it reasonable?

Is anything obscure?

Is all of it understandable?

Can anything be misunderstood?

Have I read it over once more to catch the errors that I did not catch the first time?

Has it been considered from the other person's point of view?

Have I made any assumptions? If so, have I called attention to the assumptions?

Figures:

Are the FIGURES arithmetically correct?

Has each figure been inspected for reasonableness?

Is each figure confirmed by an independent estimate?

Have any digits been written obscurely?

Has the correct starting data or source information been used?

How do the figures compare with prior figures? the figures for last year? the figures the last time the calculation was made?

Does the description of the figures specify precisely what they are?

Has the source of the figures been stated?

Has the calculation been made precisely in accordance with the instructions?

22 PROPOSITIONS RELATING TO INPUT, PROCESSING, AND OUTPUT

Common Sayings or Time-Honored Sayings:

Garbage in, garbage out. —Common saying in the computer field. But it is not universally true: what comes out may by luck or approximation be right or acceptable.

Forewarned is forearmed.

A false proposition implies any proposition. —Bertrand Russell.

When the blind lead the blind, both shall fall into the ditch. —Thomas Carlyle.

Fools rush in where angels fear to tread. —Alexander Pope.

If it be the right way, advance; if it be the wrong way, retire. —Lao Tze.

Don't throw out the baby with the bathwater.

The things which hurt, instruct. —Benjamin Franklin.

Man approaches the truth through a succession of errors. —Aldous Huxley.

Other Sayings:

The world is more complicated than most of our theories make it out to be.

Be ready to change your mind on good evidence.

A vast amount of time and effort is wasted on solving the wrong problems.

Half the work of producing a correct answer is in phrasing the correct question.

Many difficult problems are solved by a series of solutions from simple cases to complex cases, and the series of solutions teaches the solvers.

If a method of solving a problem has failed six times out of six, it is time to change your method.

Always look for signs, clues, guesses, impressions; they may lead to a discovery.

Look carefully for additional aspects to a problem: they may turn out to be important.

Try to find out the range of values of each of the input variables.

Try to estimate (without benefit of computer) the range of values of each of the output variables.

A good method for reducing one hazard may increase other hazards.

Establishments have nasty methods for hurting whistle-blowers: so try to use regular organization channels.

Cultivate a tentative viewpoint.

43 HUMAN SOURCES OF ERROR

Many very human actions cause many very human errors, for all computer installations involve people (operators, programmers, systems analysts, managers, guards, cleaning ladies and gentlemen, and top executives) and they are all human beings with all the power that human beings have for producing errors.

Failure of Perception:
  Failure to observe
  Failure to recognize

Failure to listen carefully
Failure to interpret carefully
Failure to understand

Failures of Thought Processes:
  Failure to discover the right problem
  Failure to determine all the factors and select the relevant ones
  Neglect of common ordinary knowledge
  Neglect of scientific knowledge
  Neglect of technical knowledge

  Neglect of hazards and dangers
  Neglect of the recommendations of experts
  Failure to evaluate and appraise the recommendations of experts
  Failure to use imagination
  Failure to use initiative

  Failure to study experience and derive lessons from it
  Failure to apply feedback
  Failure to plan sensibly so as to produce a timely solution
  Failure to modify plans when appropriate
  Neglect of alternative solutions

  Failure to judge sensibly
  Failure to examine all available resources and make use of them appropriately
  Failure to estimate beforehand and compare actual results with estimated results
  Neglect of logical reasoning
  Neglect of mathematical calculation

Failures from Emotions and Mind-Sets:
  Ignorance
  Inattention
  Forgetting
  Laziness
  Carelessness

  Excessive carefulness
  Placidity
  Irritability
  Stubbornness
  Prejudice and bias

Vacillation
Habit
Addictions (to drugs, alcohol, etc.)
Inattention to possible camouflage
Neglect of possible deception

101 CAUSES OF ERRORS IN COMPUTER APPLICATIONS

EXTERNAL CAUSES
Building damage: from earthquake, lightning, tornadoes, hurricanes,...
Fire damage
Flood damage
Hardware failure: main frame, peripheral devices, communication lines,...
Messages: garbled during electrical transmission, lost or destroyed physically in transit, misunderstood during verbal communication or written communication, etc.
Input data incorrect: "garbage in, garbage out"
Operating system failure
Power failure
Rodent damage: rats, squirrels,...
Software failure: program bugs,...

CAUSES RELATED TO PEOPLE: HONEST AND INTELLIGENT
Absence of choice among a wider set of alternatives
Analysis of failure:
  incomplete analysis
  not seeing all relevant factors
  not asking all relevant questions
  not defining appropriate objectives,...
Concentration failure:
  momentary inattention
  spell of inattention
  slip of the mind
  selection of the wrong formula
  adoption of the wrong assumptions
Feedback failure:
  not searching for all the lessons

not applying all the lessons
not learning from experience
not applying iteration
Ignorance:
  in general
  of a special field by a generalist
  of a general field by a specialist
Interpretation failure:
  of observations
  of facts
  jumping to conclusions
Illogic: ("I reasoned wrong," "I added wrong")
Overestimating
  of one's own knowledge
  of one's own capacity
  of the knowledge or capacity of one's own experts
Perception failure: ("I didn't notice," "I did not watch")
Precedents: ("There was no precedent")
Rules: ("I didn't apply the rule")
Testing failure:
  not testing even once
  not testing at least several cases
  not testing in a systematic yet random way
  not testing according to guidelines
Understanding failure (misunderstanding)
Vagueness: failure to verify the precise application of vague legislative or managerial specifications

CAUSES RELATED TO PEOPLE: OTHER KINDS
Criminality:
  dishonest and disloyal (wants wealth by fair means or foul)
  borderline dishonest and disloyal ("they will never miss that," "it's just a little sin," "it's like taking a wooden pencil home")
Deception: covering up, afraid to tell the truth, concealing important information
Disaffection: disgruntled, prejudiced, harboring grievances, resentful of authority

Dishonesty: person dishonest but not criminal:
  practical joker
  cracking passwords for "fun"
  stealing long distance calls for "fun"
Disloyalty:
  reading on company time
  idling by the coffee machine
  gossiping and chatting to excess
Language disability:
  person unwilling to explain
  person unable to express simple ideas in plain ordinary language
Laxity:
  content with sloppy work
  tolerant of little mistakes
  inspects and initials without inspecting
Sickness (temporary disability):
  at work but without enough sleep
  at work but too full of lunch
  had two cocktails at lunch
  worried about family problems
  ill, feverish, and should not be at work
Sickness (rather permanent disability):
  alcoholic
  on drugs
  lazy because of medical troubles
Unfriendliness:
  chip on shoulder
  unwilling to explain
  contemptuous of users or customers
  priesthood attitude re computer progamming
  eager to use jargon to confuse the manager

12 APHORISMS REGARDING THINKING

It is remarkable how long misleading or outworn beliefs survive.

The superstitions of today are the cherished beliefs of yesterday; and the cherished beliefs of today are likely to become the superstitions of tomorrow.

Many of us worship machinery as fervently as our primitive ancestors worshiped sticks and stones.

Even when a change has become inevitable, traces of old habits of thought survive; if you look at prints of the first railway carriages, you will see how similar they were to the superseded stagecoaches.

When an institution has existed unchallenged for many generations, it acquires a halo of sanctity: even the calendar and the clock.

When our old beliefs are challenged, we chant in chorus the old cant phrases, and we become angry and pugnacious.

Habits must be overhauled from time to time.

He that will not reason is a bigot; he that cannot reason is a fool; and he that dares not reason is a slave.

Thinking has been the secret of some of the greatest successes.

Great thoughts may rise from the heart, but they must go round by the head.

When we embark on a risky job, we should not simply trust to luck—but instead take all the precautions that common sense and foresight require.

We don't always believe that truth is a paying proposition—and so we take the line of least resistance and stick to the grooves of our habits.

(Source: pp 8 to 18 in *Teach Yourself to Think* by R.W. Jepson, published by English Universities Press, London, England, 1938, 164pp)

7 AXIOMS FOR EXPLANATION

Almost nobody understands the first time.

Almost nobody reads more than one page.

Nobody reads the fine print, even when writ large.

People like examples spoken.

People like examples on paper even more.

People like examples that have happened, that run on a computer, most of all.

To be impatient, to show irritation at lack of understanding, is a splendid highway to failure and defeat.

10 QUESTIONS FOR CHECKING YOUR ORGANIZATION'S EXPOSURE TO COMPUTER FRAUD AND COMPUTER CRIME

Initiating Transactions:
Are data processing employees prohibited from initiating original accounting transactions, adjustments, or corrections?

Key Personnel:
Have you identified individual programmers and other technical personnel who are in a position to inflict significant harm, or on whom your organization is unusually dependent?

Access:
Is access to your computer room, tape library, disk library, and forms storage areas denied to personnel who have no business need for access?

Scheduled Vacation:
Do employees take scheduled vacations, which can provide an opportunity to expose unauthorized practices?

Formal Procedure for Changes:
Do you use a formal procedure, which requires individual signature authorizations, for changes or modifications of software that affect systems applications?

Decoy Names:
Do your files of customers and clients contain secret decoy names and addresses so as to detect unauthorized use of those files?

Solitary Work:
As a general rule, do you prohibit anyone from working alone in the computer room?

Audit Trail:
For all major financial applications, is there a diagram and a description of an audit trail, which shows how an individual transaction can be traced through the system?

Standardized Reports of Discrepancies:
Does your internal auditing function or your security function receive standardized reports of (1) differences in cash and inventory, (2) high-dollar transactions, (3) large usages of inventory, and (4) any other unusual or inconsistent figures and activities?

Prosecution:
Would you prosecute an employee found guilty of a serious premeditated criminal act against your organization?

35 COMMON PROPERTIES AND RELATIONS OF IDEAS

Suppose you seek to explain X to a group of people who understand Y. Then you have to produce an explanation which tells the important properties and relations of X in words that are understood by people who understand Y.

For example, to explain computers to a group of senior professors of English literature is much harder than to explain computers to a group of young people who have played video games, and to explain computers to people who have been working in the computer field for a year is unnecessary.

Explanation therefore varies enormously. Usually an explainer has to use words and language. Often he can use diagrams and sketches., Sometimes he can use pictures, mathematics, movies, etc. Rarely he can use actual experiences such as field trips, interning in a hospital, etc. Regularly, in teaching a job, the explainer can use examples of doing the job, supplemented by words; this is an excellent explanation.

In explaining anything at all, it is useful to have a reminder checklist based on all the common properties and relations of anything whatever. It does not make sense to tell unimportant details until you have told important details. Following is such a checklist.

Name, identification
Other names, repetition in other words, equivalents
Examples, instances
Definition, meaning, significance
Essence, theme, nature

Kind, sort, genus, species, class
Properties, nature, habits
Similar things, related things, associated things
Opposites, contrasts
Distinguishing characteristics

Things, included in it, parts
Things of which it is a part
Context, environment, situation, field
Composition, material, substance
Structure, organization, construction

Activity, behavior, verb
Agents, doers, subject of verb
Products, object of verb, recipients
Manner, ways, adverbs
Size, dimension, measurements

Quantity, number
Variation, range, average, deviations
Shape, form, solid, liquid or gas
Weight, density
Appearance, look, color, luster

Sound, smell, taste, feel
Place, location, position, extent, prevalence
Time, duration, age, persistence

History, origin, causes, development
Future, results, effects, predictions
Purpose, function, use, worth, value
Advantages
Disadvantages
Owners, users
Importance, relation to human affairs

10 RULES FOR GOOD WRITING

Short words are better than long.

Short sentences are better than long.

Short paragraphs are better than long.

Short articles are better than long.

Direct statement is better than indirect.

The active mood is better than the passive.

Don't pussyfoot.

Be simple, human, and concise — not complex, pompous, and verbose.

Don't overwork "is", "was", and other parts of "to be".

To gain power, chop off Latin roots wherever Anglo-Saxon words can tell the same story. Thus "They considered it improbable that circumstances would permit him to divulge the occurrence," would better be, "They didn't think he had a chance to tell the news."

Those who can write by these rules when they want to, can best be trusted to break them wisely.

(Source: "Giving Power to Words" by Philip W. Swain, in *American Journal of Physics,* vol. 13, no. 5, October 1945, pp 318-320)

22 PRINCIPLES FOR SPEAKING, EXPLAINING, ARGUING, AND PERSUADING

Audience:
  Consider your audience all the time; they are looking at their wrist watches, eager to leave.
  Start a fire in the first sentence. It wakes them up, gets them interested and excited.
  Tell them why the subject is important to them.

Substance:
  Have something worth saying; say it; and stop.
  If it is necessary to say something more, say that and stop once more.
  Most people cannot take in very much at once.

Examples:
  Use examples.
  Make the examples both interesting and significant.
  Use real and not make-believe examples.
  Examples are excellent opportunities to show that some problem really exists.
  Examples are good opportunities to prove points.
  Examples are good opportunities to demonstrate applications.
  Don't choose examples that supply handles to your opponents to upset your applecart.
  Make your examples practical.

Analogies:
  Use analogies that are vivid, stimulating, exciting.
  Use analogies if possible from common experience.

Repetition:
  Repeat ideas and propositions "in other words"; most people need multiple repetitions, paraphrases.

Conclusions:
  State the conclusions you want your audience to draw.
  Say them a second time in different words.

Rebuttal Ahead of Time:
  Anticipate objections.
  State them as well as you can from the other person's point of view.
  Rebut them calmly, logically, convincingly, diplomatically.

8 Computers and Programming, Algorithms, Genius, . . .

THE PROMISE OF MACHINES THAT THINK

To me, the most exciting of all the vistas of computers is the promise of thinking, the promise contained in the developing capacity of an ever faster and more powerful computer to be able to handle reasonably the most complex thoughts that humanity can conceive of. Thinking in a computer is programming.

My first book, published in 1949, was entitled *Giant Brains or Machines that Think*. It was clear to me then that all the processes of mathematics, logic and reason underlying thinking in every field could be expressed with pencil and paper, and therefore they could be expressed with the hardware and software of computers.

The clue to this future avenue is evident in computer programming. The time will come when every thought that man can think will be a thought that a machine can think. Programming in plain ordinary natural language will become fully acceptable to machines. Learning from examples as human beings do, learning from analogies as human beings do, learning from experience as human beings do, will all be accomplished by automatic machines, by computers.

All the mistakes in life that human beings commonly make for lack of hard thinking will become curable as human beings learn more and more how to use the powers of computers. Just as the telephone has made a truly enormous change in the lives of almost everybody, so the capacity to think reasonably and accurately by means of a computer at our elbow, will transform all our lives.

53

11 PRINCIPLES REGARDING ALGORITHMS

Definition: An algorithmic activity is a procedure for carrying out a task.

Prevalence: The real and abstract worlds are continually setting forth tasks to be done.

Property: The variety is endless.

Quantity: The procedures for carrying them out appear to be endless.

Property: These procedures appear to encompass all human activity.

Subclass: We can focus our attention on an important subset of these tasks.

Definition: This subset is transformations of sequences of symbols.

Example 1: Reverse the order of the symbols in a sequence, like ABCD to DCBA.

Example 2: Combine two sequences of digits into a third sequence, in which the rule is X plus Y equals Z (say).

Example 3: Interrogating information organized into a list, file, or table.

Principle: If any external communication is required, every algorithmic task is given symbolic representation in a language.

A way by which CONDITIONS can be decided.

A way of BRANCHING from one sequence of instructions to another sequence of instructions.

A way of CYCLING or LOOPING over and over again through a sequence of instructions, with minor changes, until the cycles are finished with (otherwise we have an "infinite loop" as it is called, and the program will never come to a stop).

A way of calling SUBROUTINES or RULES for use in various kinds of cases, and then returning to the MAIN program.

A way of outputting results from time to time, to a TERMINAL or a PRINTER or a DISPLAY or a FILE or a TABLE.

A way of STOPPING.

A way of FILING the program so that it can be used again.

A way of RUNNING the program on cases and examples.

A way of MODIFYING the program to remove errors called BUGS and to take in changes in the requirements that the procedure is to meet.

13 SUBDIVISIONS OF A COMPUTER PROGRAM

A NAME by means of which it is known and can be talked about.

A way in which DATA or information can be inserted into the program.

A way by which data from a FILE or TABLE can be inserted into the program.

A way by which directions for COMPUTING and REASONING can be given to the program.

30 PROGRAMS FOR FINANCIAL CONTROL AND ANALYSIS

Simple Bookkeeping System
   posting journal entries
   trial balance
   income statement
   balance sheet
   closing accounts
   account file print
   account displaying and correction
   journal print
   income and expense comparison

Accounts Receivable System
  accounts receivable processing
  accounts receivable — reports

General Financial Programs
  breakeven analysis
  financial support programs
  income statement preparation
  balance sheet preparation
  cash flow and budget analysis
  income and expense analysis
  least-squares regression forecasting
  moving-average forecasting
  exponential-smoothing forecasting
  ratio analysis
  equipment comparisons
  depreciation
  expected value computation
  amortization
  return on investment
  property comparisons
  job pricing/bidding
  mortgage computation
  mortgage comparison program

20 PROBLEMS FOR STUDENTS OF ALGORITHMS AND PROGRAMMING

Hyphenating / hyphenating a word when putting part of it on one line and the rest of it on the next line

Spelling / a word, given its sounds and the sequence of sounds

Knitting / a garment, etc.

Cooking / some dish, according to a recipe

Syllables / counting the number of syllables in a word, a sentence, or a paragraph

Wrong Instructions / correcting instructions that are wrong, incomplete, ambiguous, etc.

Right Justification / right justifying a line of text, where different letters have different spacing, ranging from 2 points for "i" to 5 points for "W"

Spelling Correction / correcting the spelling of misspelled words as in "seperate" for "separate"

Spelling Correction / correcting the spelling of words that sound alike but that have different meanings, such as "there, their"

Recognition / how to recognize from facial features a person whom you have never seen

Identification / how to identify keys on a keychain according to their notches, slots, etc.

Plant Identification / how to identify a plant according to its properties

Meeting / how to meet a person at a place strange to both persons, who have never seen each other before

Four Fours / given any number N from 1 to 1000; and the operations of arithmetic, adjacency, etc.: express the number N as a function of four fours; example: 300 equals 4 to the 4th power plus 44

Arrest / how to proceed when you are arrested by a policeman

Survival / how to survive when you are lost in a wilderness probably at least 20 miles from the nearest help

Finding / how to find something which is lost, such as a baseball in a sandlot, or a paper in a dozen file drawers

Travel / how to give instructions for travel as, for example, to a motorist who is hunting for a street and number

Fire Prevention / how to give instructions to prevent fires in a house

Buying / how to give instructions for not purchasing useless articles or services

10 IMPORTANT POWERFUL PROGRAMMING LANGUAGES

COBOL / from "common business-oriented programming language"

FORTRAN / from "formula translation"

BASIC / from "basic all-purpose symbolic language for integrating and calculating", or "beginners' all-purpose symbolic instruction code"

ALGOL / from "algorithmic language"

LISP / from "list processing"

BAL / from "basic assembly language" (IBM 360)

APL / from "a programming language"

ADA / in honor of Augusta Ada Byron (1816-51)

PASCAL / in honor of Blaise Pascal (1623-62)

PL/I / from "programming language I"

308 RESERVE WORDS OF THE PROGRAMMING LANGUAGE COBOL

ACCEPT
ACCESS
ADD
ADVANCING
AFTER
ALL
ALPHABETIC
ALSO
ALTER
ALTERNATE
AND
ARE
AREA
AREAS
ASCENDING
ASSIGN
AT

AUTHOR
BEFORE
BLANK
BLOCK
BOTTOM
BY
CALL
CANCEL
CD
CF
CH
CHARACTER
CHARACTERS
CLOCK-UNITS
CLOSE
COBOL
CODE
CODE-SET
COLLATING
COLUMN
COMMA
COMMUNICATION
COMP
COMPUTATIONAL
COMPUTE
CONFIGURATION
CONTAINS
CONTROL
CONTROLS
COPY
CORR
CORRESPONDING
COUNT
CURRENCY

DATA
DATE
DATE-COMPILED
DATE-WRITTEN
DAY
DE
DEBUG-CONTENTS
DEBUG-ITEM
DEBUG-NAME
DEBUG-SUB-1
DEBUG-SUB-2
DEBUG-SUB-3
DEBUGGING

DECIMAL-POINT
DECLARATIVES
DELETE
DELIMITED
DELIMITER
DEPENDING
DESCENDING
DESTINATION
DETAIL
DISABLE
DISPLAY
DIVIDE
DIVISION
DOWN
DUPLICATES
DYNAMIC

EGI
ELSE
EMI
ENABLE
END
END-OF-PAGE
ENTER
ENVIRONMENT
EOP
EQUAL
ERROR
ESI
EVERY
EXCEPTION
EXIT
EXTEND

FD
FILE
FILE-CONTROL
FILLER
FINAL
FIRST
FOOTING
FOR
FROM

GENERATE
GIVING
GO
GREATER
GROUP

HEADING
HIGH-VALUE
HIGH-VALUES
I-O
I-O–CONTROL
IDENTIFICATION
IF
IN
INDEX
INDEXED
INDICATE
INITIAL
INITIATE
INPUT
INPUT-OUTPUT
INSPECT
INSTALLATION
INTO
INVALID
IS

JUST
JUSTIFIED

KEY

LABEL
LAST
LEADING
LEFT
LENGTH
LESS
LIMIT
LIMITS
LINAGE
LINAGE-COUNTER
LINE
LINE-COUNTER
LINES
LINKAGE
LOCK
LOW-VALUE
LOW-VALUES

MEMORY
MERGE
MESSAGE
MODE
MODULES
MOVE

MULTIPLE
MULTIPLY

NATIVE
NEGATIVE
NEXT
NO
NOT
NUMBER
NUMERIC

OBJECT-COMPUTER
OCCURS
OF
OFF
OMITTED
ON
OPEN
OPTIONAL
OR
ORGANIZATION
OUTPUT
OVERFLOW

PAGE
PAGE-COUNTER
PERFORM
PF
PH
PIC
PICTURE
PLUS
POINTER
POSITION
POSITIVE
PRINTING
PROCEDURE
PROCEDURES
PROCEED
PROGRAM
PROGRAM-ID

QUEUE
QUOTE
QUOTES

RANDOM
RD
READ
RECEIVE
RECORD

RECORDS
REDEFINES
REEL
REFERENCES
RELATIVE
RELEASE
REMAINDER
REMOVAL
RENAMES
REPLACING
REPORT
REPORTING
REPORTS
RERUN
RESERVE
RESET
RETURN
REVERSED
REWIND
REWRITE
RF
RH
RIGHT
ROUNDED
RUN

SAME
SD
SEARCH
SECTION
SECURITY
SEGMENT
SEGMENT-LIMIT
SELECT
SEND
SENTENCE
SEPARATE
SEQUENCE
SEQUENTIAL
SET
SIGN
SIZE
SORT
SORT-MERGE
SOURCE
SOURCE-COMPUTER
SPACE
SPACES

SPECIAL-NAMES
STANDARD
STANDARD-1
START
STATUS
STOP
STRING
SUB-QUEUE-1
SUB-QUEUE-2
SUB-QUEUE-3
SUBTRACT
SUM
SUPPRESS
SYMBOLIC
SYNC
SYNCHRONIZED

TABLE
TALLYING
TAPE
TERMINAL
TERMINATE
TEXT
THAN
THROUGH
THRU
TIME
TIMES
TO
TOP
TRAILING

TYPE
UNIT
UNSTRING
UNTIL
UP
UPON
USAGE
USE
USING
VALUE
VALUES
VARYING

WHEN
WITH
WORDS
WORKING-STORAGE
WRITE

ZERO
ZEROES
ZEROS

+
−
*
/
**
>
<
=

113 KEYWORDS OF THE PROGRAMMING LANGUAGE CBASIC AND GUIDE TO THEIR MEANINGS

Key Word	Meaning
ABS(X)	the absolute value of the argument X
AND	logical AND
AS	assigns an identification number to the file being opened
ASC(A$)	the ASCII numerical value in decimal of the first character of A$
ATN(X)	the arc tangent of X in radians

BUFF	specifies the number of disk sectors
CALL	links to a machine language subroutine
CBASIC	invokes the CBASIC compiler to compile a source file written in CBASIC (filetype BAS) giving an intermediate file (filetype INT)
%CHAIN	chain statement to chain programs; compiler directive
CHR$ (I%)	a one character string whose ASCII value is I%
CLOSE	closes a file that has been opened
COMMAND$	returns a string which contains part of the CP/M command line
CONCHAR$	reads one character from the console
CONSOLE	restores printed output to the console
CONSTAT%	console status
COS(X)	the cosine of X in radians
CREATE	opens a new file
CRUN	runs an intermediate file (filetype INT)
DATA	defines constants which are assigned to variables by READ statements
DEF	signal for definition of a function name
DELETE	removes a referenced file
DIM	dimension
%EJECT	sets a form feed; compiler directive
ELSE	part of the IF . . . THEN . . . ELSE statement
EQ	equal to
EXP(X)	the constant e = 2.718 . . . raised to the power X
FEND	signal for the end of a multiple line function name
FILE	opens a file if present, otherwise creates a file
FLOAT(I%)	converts I% to a real value
FN	prefix of a function name of a user defined function
FOR	part of a FOR . . . TO . . . NEXT statement
FOR . . . TO . . . STEP . . .	execute all statements until the exit criteria are met
FRE	number of bytes of unused space in free storage
GE	greater than or equal to
GO	execution continues at the statement labeled with the GOTO

GOSUB	go to subroutine and return to next line number
GOTO	execution continues at the statement labeled with the GOTO
IF	a part of the IF statement
IF . . . THEN	a form of the IF statement
IF . . . THEN . . . ELSE	the regular form of the IF statement
%INCLUDE	compiler directive; includes another program to be compiled together
INP	returns the value input from the I/O port
INPUT	returns prompt string or ?, then a line of input data read
INITIALIZE	initialize the disk system
INT	filetype INTERMEDIATE, produced by compilation of a CBASIC source program with filetype BAS
INT(X)	the integer part of the argument
INT%(X)	converts the argument X to an integer value
LE	less than or equal to
LEFT$(A$,I%)	returns a string of the first I% characters of A$
LEN(A$)	the length of A$ in characters
LET	the expression is evaluated and assigned to the variable
LINE	refers to lines of files; see READ statement
%LIST	compiler directive; sets "listing" on
LOCAL	?
LOG(X)	the natural logarithm of X
LPRINTER	sets output to the listing printer
LT	less than
MATCH(A$,B$,I%)	the first position of the first occurrence of A$ in B$ starting with the character position I%
MID$(A$,I%,J%)	returns a string of the J% characters of A$ starting with the character position I%
NE	not equal to
NEXT	denotes end of closest unmatched FOR statement
%NOLIST	compiler directive; sets "no listing" on
NOT	logical NOT
ON	sets a line number at which execution will continue
ON . . . GOSUB	sets a line number at which execution will continue

ON . . . GOTO	sets a line number at which execution will continue
OPEN	activates an existing file for opening or updating
OR	logical OR, inclusive
OUT	low order 8 bits sent to the output port
%PAGE	handles pages; compiler directive
PEEK	returns content of the memory location of the expression
POKE X, Y	stores the low order 8 bits of Y at the memory address selected by X
POS	current position of the pointer in the buffer of the output line
PRINT	outputs values of the expression to the console or lister
PRINT	outputs data to disk files; four styles
PRINT USING	print using a format string
RANDOMIZE	seeds the random number generator
READ	assigns values from DATA statements to the variables
READ	accesses data from files; four styles
RECL	record length in bytes
RECS	specifies number of bytes in a sector; normally 128
REM	a remark
REMARK	a remark
RENAME(A$,B$)	changes at once the name of the file B$ to the new name A$
RESTORE	repositions pointer into the data area, so that the next value read will be the first item in the data statement
RETURN	returns to the next address after the GOSUB
RIGHT$(A$,I%)	returns a string of the I% rightmost characters of A$
RND	generates a uniformly distributed random number between 0 and 1
SADD%	the address of the string assigned to A$
SAVEMEM	saves machine language memory
SGN(X)	−1 if X is negative, 0 if X is zero, +1 if X is positive
SIN(X)	the sine of X in radians
SIZE(A$)	the size in blocks of file A$
SQR(X)	the square root of X
STEP	part of FOR . . . TO . . . STEP . . . statement
STOP	stops the program

STR$(X)	returns the character string representing the value of the number X
SUB	part of GOSUB; subroutine call
TAB(X)	repositions output buffer pointer to the position X
TAN(X)	the tangent of X in radians
THEN	part of the IF . . . THEN . . . ELSE . . . statement
TO	part of GO TO and FOR . . . TO, which see
TRACE	TRACE option for run time debugging
UCASE$	translates lower case characters in A$ into upper case
USING	part of PRINT USING, which see
VAL(A$)	converts A$ into a floating point number
WEND	end of the closest unmatched WHILE
WHILE	executes all statements between the WHILE statement and the corresponding WEND until . . . is zero
WIDTH	sets the line width on the list device
XOR	logical EXCLUSIVE OR
XREF	cross reference lister

24 CHARACTERISTICS OF THE PERSONALITY OF A HUMAN GENIUS

Drive and Perseverence: Geniuses have a strong desire to work hard and long.

Courage: They have the courage to do things that others consider impossible.

Goal-Centered: Geniuses know what they want and go after it.

Knowledge: They continually accumulate knowledge, information, answers to questions.

Frankness: They are frank, forthright, honest, responsible, admit mistakes, and learn from their mistakes.

Optimism: They never doubt they will succeed.

Judgment: They try to understand the facts in a situation before they judge, yet they are willing to change their minds.

Enthusiasm: They are enthusiastic about what they are doing, and infect others with their enthusiasm.

Willing to Take Chances: They are willing to take chances.

Energy and Push: They don't wait for some desired thing to happen — they push.

Opportunity-Seeking: They seek opportunities, take on tasks that others won't touch.

Persuasion and Motivation: They know how to persuade and motivate other people.

Outgoing: They make friends easily, and don't abuse their friendships.

Communicative: They are able to get their ideas across to others.

Patience: They are patient with others, impatient with themselves.

Perceptive: They are perceptive.

Perfectionism: They do not tolerate mediocrity, never in themselves.

Sense of Humor: They are willing to laugh at their own blunders.

Versatile: They are versatile.

Adaptable: They are adaptable, flexible.

Curiosity: They are inquisitive, always curious.

Individualism: They do things the way they think those things should be done, without much regard for convention or precedent.

Idealism: They strive to achieve great things, not for themselves, but for all humanity.

Imagination: They think in new combinations, new directions, "what if?"

20 CHARACTERISTICS OF A GENIUS COMPUTER PROGRAM

Drive and Perseverance / The computer program is tireless; so it has drive and perseverance.

Courage / It will do anything, no matter what the danger. It is fearless.

Goal-Centered / A computer program focuses on its goal.

Knowledge / With the help of a human, it will accept any knowledge or information.

Frankness / It will admit any mistakes (and will learn from them) if so programmed.

Optimism / It does not doubt it will succeed.

Judgment / With the help of a human it will accept any facts.

Enthusiasm / It is single-minded about what it is doing (and it influences humans to be enthusiastic).

Willing to Take Chances / It will certainly do so if so programmed.

Energy and Push / It has indefinitely much energy, and it pushes.

Opportunity-Seeking / It will seek opportunities if so programmed.

Communicative / It is able to communicate its messages to anybody.

Patience / It is always patient, far more patient than most teachers, parents, or friends.

Perceptive / It always responds to input information when machine-readable.

Perfectionism / It does not tolerate imperfection.

Versatile / It is able to do anything that it is programmed for.

Adaptable / It can adjust to a great variety of requirements.

Curiosity / It can be continuously inquisitive and curious while receiving data.

Individualistic / It can be programmed to do a task without reference to conventions or precedents.

Imagination / It can seek exploration and recombination of ideas unlimitedly.

16 HUMAN GENIUSES

Confucius (K'ung Fu-tzu) (551?–479? BC) / Chinese philosopher

Euripides (480?–406? BC) / Greek dramatist; he wrote 52 tragedies, acted them in Athens

Aristotle (384–322 BC) / Greek teacher, philosopher, writer

Archimedes (287?–242 BC) / Greek mathematician, inventor, physicist

Leonardo da Vinci (1452–1519) / Florentine painter, sculptor, architect, engineer

William Shakespeare (1564–1616) / English dramatist, poet

Galileo Galilei (1564–1642) / Italian physicist, astronomer

Isaac Newton (1642–1727) / English mathematician, scientist

Voltaire (Francois-Marie Arouet) (1694–1778) / French lawyer, writer

Benjamin Franklin (1706–1790) / American statesman, philosopher, scientist

Wolfgang Amadeus Mozart (1756–1791) / Austrian musical composer

Karl Friedrich Gauss (1777–1855) / German mathematician, astronomer

Charles Darwin (1809–1882) / English naturalist, scientist; he proposed the evolution of species

Louis Pasteur (1822–1895) / French chemist and scientist; he founded bacteriology, demonstrated a cure for rabies

Bertrand Russell (1872–1969) / English mathematician, philosopher, author

Albert Einstein (1879–1955) / American (German-born) physicist, scientist; he proposed the theory of relativity

9 Computers and Language, Discussion, Communication, Symbols...

BEHAVIOR THAT CHANGES ACCORDING TO EXPERIENCE OR INSTRUCTIONS

A fundamental property of a computer is that it can handle flexible sequences of reasonable operations on information. Inflexible sequences can be handled by washing machines, cuckoo clocks, automatic pumps, and so on. But flexibility implies differing responses to differing conditions and differing content of memory (such as more experience), and so behavior changes according to experience or instructions or both.

Inside its "skin" or boundary, a computer possesses an internal language of binary coding, that is, one's and zero's, or on-ness and off-ness of switches, or presence or absence of pulses, and so on. Packages of binary digits are sent from any part to a host of other parts, conveying messages and ideas. An idea is the meaning common to a set of symbols which have the same meaning: "sum", "add", "plus", "totaling" and some other words all contain the idea "+". That idea can be built with gears into the hardware of an adding machine, or can be represented in the behavior of a computer by a sequence of bits.

Outside the skin or boundary of a computer are a vast number of external languages. Spoken English is a collection of words, phrases, sentences, intonations, sound-waves, etc., used by more than 300 million people. The physical equipment for spoken English consists of the voices of people for transmitting, and the ears of people for receiving. There are more than 1500 living languages and over 3000 dead languages among human beings, as well as over 100 languages among bees, ants, dogs, wolves, dolphins, whales, crows, jackdaws, and other animals. For example, baring the teeth (a sight) and growling (a sound) are expressive gestures of language for thousands of species of animals all over the world.

7 MEANINGS OF THE WORD "LANGUAGE"

The aspect of human behavior that involves vocal sounds in meaningful patterns and, when they exist, corresponding written symbols to form, express, and communicate thoughts and feelings

A historically established pattern of such behavior that offers substantial communication only within the culture it defines: "the English language"

Any method of communicating ideas, as by a system of signs, symbols, gestures, and the like: "the language of algebra"

The transmission of meaning, feeling, or intent by significance of act or manner

The special vocabulary and usages of a group

A characteristic style of speech or writing

The manner or means of communication between living creatures other than man: "the language of dolphins"

5 MEANINGS OF THE WORD "INFORMATION"

Factual, such as we find in:
encyclopedias
textbooks
telephone books
timetables

Suppositions, such as we find in:
novels
fables

fairy tales
jokes

Biased reports and special pleadings:
communiques from generals
speeches of politicians
addresses to juries
denials of diplomats

Collections of marks that have meaning:
letters of the alphabet
decimal digits
typewriter signs like @
punctuation marks like '

Cryptographic messages like:
enciphered texts
codes using a code book
ancient writing with the key lost
Stonehenge, Angkor Wat,...

9 TYPES OF HUMAN LANGUAGE

Age Beginning	Type of Language
1 month	deeds and interpretation
2 months	gesture and behavior
9 months	watching and imitating
1 and ½ years	expressions using one spoken word
2 years	expressions using two spoken words
4 years	many spoken words and many sentences
5 years	over 5000 spoken words
8	reading for fun
12	reading and writing for work and fun

(Note: The "age beginning" is approximate only; human beings do not lose any of these 9 languages once acquired, until senility or death)

12 PRINCIPAL LANGUAGES OF THE WORLD

Language	Number of Speakers (millions)
Mandarin	690
English	380
Russian	259
Spanish	238
Hindi	230
Arabic	142
Portuguese	141
Bengali	140
German	120
Japanese	115
Malay-Indonesian	106
French	100

CEMENT WORDS

An important division of the common words that everybody uses over and over again every day consists of the "cement words", the little words which (like the cement surrounding bricks) appear in nearly all discussion, conversation, and arguments that are expressed in English. These are the commonest words in English, such as "the, of, and, to, a, in, is, for, ..."

We contrast these words with the "brick words," words which (like the bricks that construct a building) belong specifically to some context, such as:

food: eggs, bread, cheese, milk, cook, eat, ...

chess: king, queen, rook, pawn, castling, en passant, ...

traveling: bus, driver, seat, ticket, car, flight, pilot ....

If a computer is to compute the answer to a question expressed in words, or the reasonable solution to an argument expressed in words, then the computer should be able to recognize and "understand" easily the meanings of cement words and their relations and combinations. A computer should do this just as it understands 2, 3.1416, EQUAL, REMARK and all the English and mathematical words which thousands of programmed computers already understand. It should perform this helpful function at least a hundred times faster than a human being, and far more reliably.

It is convenient to recognize four classes of cement words grouped under:

language, communication, and discussion

science in general (including time)

mathematics (including space), and

logic

The cement words of discussion fill our ears day after day. Let us listen to some of them:

What do you think about that?

I would agree.

I don't understand you.

What did you say?

I don't know what you are talking about.

He's always asking questions.

Following is a list of some of the cement words of language, communication, and discussion. Basically, these cement words express relations between persons and information.

140 CEMENT WORDS OF LANGUAGE, COMMUNICATION, AND DISCUSSION

Speakers: I, my, mine, me, we, us, our, ours

Listeners: you, your, yours

Persons or Things Spoken of: he, him, his, she, her, hers, it, its, they, them, their, theirs, who? what? which? whom? whose? how? why?

Transmitting Communication: ask, say, said, tell, told, speak, spoke, call, talk, voice, sound

Receiving Communications: listen, read

Having Knowledge: know, understand

Not Having Knowledge: don't know, don't understand

Acquiring Knowledge: find out, discover, learn, invent

Losing Knowledge: forget, don't remember

Referring to Knowledge: remember, recollect, look up

Manipulating Knowledge: consider, think, study, think about, find, thought, knowledge, realize, opinion, idea, understanding, subject

Putting Out Knowledge: say, write, tell, inform, express, reply, print, pen, pencil

Items or Production of Knowledge: word, letter, term, phrase, idea, statement, page, message, story, note, answer, questions, news, speech, language, demand, figure, paper, account, history, sentence, map, record, report, list, copy, problem, expression

Places Where Knowledge is Stored: brain, mind, memory, book

References of Words: name, mark, sign, signal, meaning, mean, sense

Attitudes about Knowledge: believe, doubt, consider, suppose, decide, opinion, guess, interesting, curious, why?

Comparing Attitudes about Knowledge: agree, argue, assert, disagree, declare, discuss, explain, explanation, claim

Surprise, Expectation: but, but then, yet, though, after all

THE 20 COMMONEST WORDS OF ONE SYLLABLE IN SEQUENCE BY FREQUENCY PER MILLION WORDS

Word	Frequency
the	69971
of	36411
and	28852
to	26149
a	23237
in	21341
that	10595
is	10099
was	9816
he	9543
for	9489
it	8756
with	7289
as	7250
his	6997
on	6742
be	6377
at	5378
by	5395
I	5173

(Source: *Computational Analysis of Present-Day American English* by H. Kucera and W. N. Francis, Brown Univ. Press, Providence, RI 02906, 2nd printing, 1970)

69

THE 20 COMMONEST WORDS OF TWO SYLLABLES IN SEQUENCE BY FREQUENCY PER MILLION WORDS

Word	Frequency
about	1815
into	1791
only	1747
other	1702
any	1345
over	1236
even	1171
after	1070
also	1069
many	1030
before	1016
because	883
people	847
little	831
between	730
being	712
under	707
never	696
against	626
himself	603

(Source: same as previous)

THE 42 COMMONEST WORDS OF THREE SYLLABLES IN SEQUENCE BY FREQUENCY PER MILLION WORDS

Word	Frequency
another	693
however	552
general	497
united	482
government	417
business	392
president	382
several	377
national	375
possible	373
important	369
interest	330
different	312
example	292
company	290
history	286
anything	280
already	273
together	267
period	265
probably	261
position	241
department	225
policy	222
following	221
century	207
Washington	206
evidence	204
various	201
personal	196
expected	187
everything	185
conditions	180
attention	179
including	171
industry	171
developed	170
committee	168
religious	165
beginning	164
difficult	161
similar	157

(Source: same as previous)

THE 36 COMMONEST WORDS OF FOUR SYLLABLES IN SEQUENCE BY FREQUENCY PER MILLION WORDS

Word	Frequency
American	569
development	334
experience	276
information	269

political	258	particularly	146
available	245	association	132
economic	243	organization	127
society	237	immediately	123
community	231	opportunity	121
necessary	222	considerable	96
education	214	possibility	87
military	212	individuals	73
situation	196	characteristic	68
America	194	intellectual	66
secretary	191	California	65
particular	179	contemporary	63
material	174	organizations	61
actually	166	interpretations	54
especially	160	administrative	53
industrial	143	characteristics	52
population	136	investigation	51
temperature	135	necessarily	51
literature	133	opportunities	51
generally	132	Philadelphia	50
apparently	125	occasionally	48
understanding	121	personality	48
additional	120	manufacturers	47
activity	116	representative	47

activity | 116
activities | 115
obviously | 114
operation | 113
democratic | 109
analysis | 108
interested | 105
professional | 105
original | 103

(Source: same as previous)

(Source: same as previous)

10 COMMONEST WORDS OF SIX SYLLABLES IN SEQUENCE BY FREQUENCY PER MILLION WORDS

Word	Frequency
responsibility	118
simultaneously	38
responsibilities	25
physiological	22
availability	21
revolutionary	21
probabilities	20
individually	19
superiority	14
experimentation	13

(Source: same as previous)

THE 28 COMMONEST WORDS OF FIVE SYLLABLES IN SEQUENCE BY FREQUENCY PER MILLION WORDS

Word	Frequency
individual	239
university	214
administration	161
international	155

10 COMPLETE UTTERANCES OF ONE WORD

Ouch!
Wow!
Hurray!
Damn!
Please.
Hello!
Perhaps.
Hush.
Stop!
Goodbye.

10 COMPLETE UTTERANCES OF 4 WORDS

The more, the merrier,
Eventually — why not now?
Will you marry me?
The die is cast.
The rich become richer.
Tiger, tiger, burning bright.
All hell broke loose.
Life is a dream.
Queen of the sciences.
Keep off the grass.

10 COMPLETE UTTERANCES OF 2 WORDS

Time flies.
Shut up!
Never mind.
Help me.
I disagree.
No smoking
One way
Main Street
Bon voyage!
Dead end

10 COMPLETE UTTERANCES OF 5 WORDS

Time flies like an arrow.
Fruit flies like a banana.
Notice flies like a dragonfly.
Judge the day at evening.
Experience is a harsh mistress.
Double, double, toil and trouble.
'Twas the night before Christmas.
Old Macdonald had a farm.
Every flow has an ebb.
Long time no talk to.

10 COMPLETE UTTERANCES OF 3 WORDS

What is is.
Circumstances alter cases.
I love you.
Veni, vidi, vici.
Each for himself.
Sauve qui peut.
More in kitchen.
Family hold back.
Never give up.
How are you?

10 COMPLETE UTTERANCES OF 6 WORDS

It is the will of Allah.
A stitch in time saves nine.
I came, I saw, I conquered.
Many and light fill the purse.
Who steals my purse steals trash.
Next station stop is Pennsylvania Station.
You can't push on a rope.
It is raining cats and dogs.
A rolling stone gathers no moss.
No stones fall from the sky.

10 COMPLETE UTTERANCES OF 7 WORDS

Who pays the piper calls the tune.
If some is good, more is better.
The rich become richer, the poor poorer.
Smoking is prohibited in this waiting room.
The mills of the gods grind slow.
The next station stop is New York.
Illumination in these premises should be extinguished.
Turn out all lights before going home.
Doctor, I am in trouble with nightmares.
Love me now ere 'tis too late.

50 ANSWERS TO QUESTIONS AND COMMENTS ON STATEMENTS

Affirmative
  Always
  Certainly
  Correct
  I agree
  No problem
  Of course
  OK
  Right
  Sure
  Surely
  That's so
  True
  Yes
  You bet
Negative
  False
  I disagree
  Never
  No
  No way
  Not at all
  Not so
  Over my dead body
  Wrong

Probability weighing
  Almost always
  Almost never
  It depends
  Maybe
  Maybe not
  Often
  Perhaps
  Perhaps not
  Probably
  Probably not
  Rarely
  Seldom
  Sometimes
Knowledge weighing
  Hunh?
  I don't know
  I don't see
  I don't understand
  I haven't decided
  I'll think about it
  I see
  I understand
  Oh!
  So that's it
Confidence weighing
  I have nothing to say
  I refuse to answer
  I stay mute
  No comment

54 WORDS OF TWO OR MORE SYLLABLES DEFINED IN ONE-SYLLABLE-WORD EQUIVALENTS

appreciate	give great worth to
condiment	spice
confound	get mixed up
consign	put in the care of
construct	make
decadent	on the down slope
decay	go bad
echo	sound that comes back
eclipse	put in the shade
effusive	full of words

elucidate	make clear
enactment	law put in force
encompass	put round, go round
epitaph	words put on a stone at one's death
grovel	go down on one's knees in front of
hallucinate	seem to see things that are not there
harangue	long talk
hereditary	handed down
hesitate	take a small time for thought
mercy	wish not to give pain
misconception	a wrong thought
mismanage	do (a thing) wrong
mistrust	have doubts in, not trust
misunderstand	get the wrong point
monarchy	rule by a king
monopoly	being just one in a field
moribund	being at the point of death
mutilate	wound and cut
nibble	take small bites
nocturnal	at night, by night
notorious	with a bad name
nucleus	small group
oblige	do a kind act
obstacle	thing in the way
occupy	take up, be in
occur	take place
offend	do wrong to, hurt
orate	talk well in front of men
ponder	give thought to
popular	liked by all, dear to all
precipice	straight drop down
prevaricate	say what is not true, dodge, tell a lie
prevent	keep from taking place
reprimand	say sharp words to
reprint	print once more
repugnant	not pleasing
resolute	free from fear
starboard	right side of ship
submit	give way to
subscribe	put one's name to
suppress	put a stop to

tremor	shake of the earth
ubiquitous	in a lot of places
worship	go down on one's knees in front of

6 MEANINGS OF THE WORD "YES", ONLY ONE OF WHICH IS BOOLEAN

yes 1   the statement is true; expresses assent or agreement; example — "Is he now happy?" "Yes, he is."

yes 2   "on the contrary"; introduces a correction or contradiction of a negative assertion; example — "Don't do that!" "Yes, I will."

yes 3   "I did not hear what you said, but I want to be polite."

yes 4   "I don't wish to disagree with you in public."

yes 5   "probably"

yes 6   "maybe; perhaps"

(Note: The Boolean meaning is the use of "yes" as meaning "true" in Boolean algebra; and persons (such as computer programmers) who think a good deal about Boolean algebra tend to forget many other meanings of "yes" as used in the common everyday world.)

14 STAGES OF THE CHARACTER AND SYMBOL B

Stage	Symbol
About 1000 B.C. Phoenicians and Semites named it "beth" meaning house	9 9 9
After 900 B.C. Greeks borrowed it, and changed name to "beta"	⅄ β B

Passed via Etruscan to the Roman alphabet	B B
Late Roman, medieval Uncial, and Cursive	B b
Modern	B ℬ b 𝒷

(Source: *The American Heritage Dictionary of the English Language,* Houghton Mifflin Company, Boston, MA, 1969, 1491)

26 LETTERS WITH NAME AND OPTIONAL SIGNS FOR MAKING CRYPTOGRAMS MORE EYE-APPEALING

Letter	Name	Sign
A	ARROW	⇧
B	BALLS	ஃ
C	CATERPILLAR	♌
D	DEL	▽
E	EYES	)•(
F	FLOWERBUD	⚘
G	GOALPOSTS	╫
H	HEART	♡
I	INSECT	Ӿ
J	JEWEL	◇
K	KEY	⊸
L	LIPS	⊖
M	MOON	☽
N	NET	⨳
O	OCTAHEDRON	⟐
P	POLE	ǂ
Q	SQUARE	■
R	RECTANGLE	▭
S	SUN	●
T	TULIP	⚕
U	ANTLERS	♈
V	HOUSE	⌂
W	WHEEL	⊙
X	EX	×
Y	PITCHFORK	Ұ
Z	ZIGZAG	Ƶ

12 PROPOSITIONS REGARDING LANGUAGE, COMMUNICATION, AND INTELLIGENCE

Insofar as the "signal code" of a species of social animal can be called a language, it can be understood by a man who has come to know its "vocabulary."

Lower and non-social animals do not have anything that could be compared with a language, for the simple reason that they do not have anything to say.

By knowing the "vocabulary" of some highly social species of beast or bird, it is often possible to attain an astonishing intimacy and mutual understanding.

How sad and mentally stunted is a caged monkey or parrot, and how incredibly alert, amusing, and interesting is the same animal in complete freedom!

The keeping of higher animals in a state of unrestricted freedom has always been my specialty.

Monkeys have an insatiable curiosity for every object that is new to them.

When I come home from my walk, these grey geese, now flying in company with wild migrants, will be standing on the steps in front of the veranda, their necks outstretched in that gesture which, in geese, means the same as tail-wagging in a dog.

It appeared to me a little short of a miracle that a hard matter-of-fact scientist had been able to establish a real friendship with wild, free-living animals.

The highly social species of birds such as the jackdaw or the greylag goose, have a complicated code of signals which are uttered and understood by every bird without any previous experience.

The mysterious apparatus for transmitting and receiving the sign stimuli which convey moods is age-old, far older than mankind itself.

I heard the jackdaws in northern Russia "talk" exactly the same, familiar "dialect" as my birds at home in Altenberg.

Jackdaws or dogs are obliged to "read in each other's eyes" what they are about to do in the next moment.

(Source: *King Solomon's Ring: New Light on Animal Ways* by Konrad Z. Lorenz, published by Thomas Y. Crowell Co., New York, 1952, 202 pp.)

4 COMPUTER POEMS

Dunetune

Leaving no footprints on water she sleeps
   with shadows prescience passed future
Starlike in youth dunelike in age my freedom
   is hers
Spacespectre walking on planets undreamed of
her eyes sing fire melodies.

Essence of dreams
Walking on planets undreamed of she awaits
   the return of waves
She remembers no one
Essence of dreams parted in some long
   forgotten seed
her eyes sing fire melodies

Born of a universal stalemate
   joining joy with repose a time for
   inconsequence my freedom is hers
Walking on planets undreamed of leaving no
   footprints on water
her eyes sing fire melodies.

Clutching at dreams I whisper her name
   clutching at dreams   her name
   dreams clutching at name her I dream
   dreams I dream clutching at clutching
   her   clutching at her
  dreams

Gus Garside and *Robin Shirley*

(Source: From *Computer Poems*, gathered by Richard W. Bailey from computer-assisted literary works executed in Britain, Canada, the Netherlands, and the United States. Copyright 1973 by Potagannissing Press, Drummond Island, Mich. Copies of *Computer Poems* (64 pp.) are available from Potagannissing Press, 1609 Cambridge Rd., Ann Arbor, MI 48104, at $2.25 each (post-paid). Excerpts reprinted with permission. Reprinted from *Computers and Automation* (subsequently *Computers and People*) for August, 1973.)

Haiku are Like Trolleys
(There'll Be Another One Along in a Moment)

Wandering in mist
reaching out to soft sunlight
blue-scaled dragons pause.

Moon low over sea
glimpse of discarded cocoon
small fish swimming idly.

Fisherman's boat drifts
meditating on lilies
fireflies listening.

Quail against water
walking and seeing woodsmoke
lonely city, dark.

White kittens playing
reaching out to plum blossoms
mist beyond riders.

Arriving in mist
thoughts of white poinsettias
snow leopards watching.

Moon low over sea
sudden vision of moonrise
white mandarin ducks.

Robert Gaskins, Jr.

(Source: same as previous)

Pavan for the Children of Deep Space

Ice worlds,
Haunted by the legend of planets. Ice worlds
  — Arcturus Andromeda Vega — orbiting,
Lost among stardust through aeons of crystal.

Your seed has dispersed, lit by the jewels
  of infinity,
Lost in the empty ocean;
In time with the measured dance of the
  universe
  orbiting . . . orbiting . . .

I am a child of eternity:
  down is a lifetime in every direction.
Through aeons of crystal your seed has
  dispersed on a journey to no destination
  sunburst starburst
  Mars Venus Jupiter Saturn . . .
Down is a lifetime in every direction.

Born out of darkness:
Lost in the palaces of eternity;
Lit by the jewels of infinity
  of the land of nowhere,
Your seed has dispersed in the dark
  light-years.
  (Sunburst starburst)

I am a child of eternity;
I travel with comets . . .
  born of some other, lost among stardust.
Lit by the jewels of infinity
  down is a lifetime in every direction.

Mars Venus Jupiter Saturn: lost
  in the empty ocean.
Orbiting: on a journey to no destination.
  . . . Procyon Eridanus Rigel . . .

Lit by the jewels of infinity,
I travel with comets.

Robin Shirley

(Source: same as previous)

Margaret

Margaret, are you saddening
Above the windy jumbles of the tide?

Wave to me in the peace of the night.
Jealousy is not all: It is not refreshment
  nor water.

Return to me in the pause of the shade,
Darling, because my spirit can chime.

Above the early flounces of the stream
Margaret, are you saddening?

Louis T. Milic

(Source: same as previous)

10 Computers and Mathematics, Numbers, Problem Solving, Strategy . . .

- Computers and Mathematics
- Mathematics, Queen of Imagination
- Variables in Office Operations
- Cement Words of Mathematics
- 14 Very Famous Numbers
- Number Words and Their Relative Frequency in English
- Computer Space Required to Store One Million Characters of Information
- Decimal Numbers Converted to 3 Other Number Scales
- Binary Addition and Multiplication
- Octal Addition and Multiplication
- Hexadecimal Addition and Multiplication
- 11 Problems in Arithmetic for Supple Minds
- 6 Properties of Prime Numbers
- 12 Classes that Have No Members at all
- 12 Classes that Have at Least a Billion Billion Members
- Principles for Solving Problems
- Principles for Solving Problems in Office Operations
- Principles of Strategy in Chess

COMPUTERS AND MATHEMATICS

The problems of mathematics and the development of mathematicians were the basic cause of computers.

The problems of dealing with numbers and other mathematical ideas compelled the Sumerians of c. 3000 BC to create a number system based on 60. Five thousand years later we still use their 24 hours, 60 minutes, and 60 seconds for measuring angles in a circle and the flow of time.

The problem of locating the boundaries of farms annually flooded by the Nile compelled the Egyptians to develop methods for measuring and surveying land. Four thousand years later we still use the 3, 4, 5 triangle which their carpenters used for making a right angle.

The challenge of adding up a column of figures more quickly and easily than his accountant father led Blaise Pascal to create in 1642 the first geared adding machine. Like the abacus, the adding machine of Pascal has had thousands of descendants.

Mathematics, Queen of Imagination

Line and circle, point and angle, space
And curvature, cosine and cosecant:
So speak the men who chart the roads, and trace
The maps of land and oceans, earth and sky.

Four point seven, naught, or minus six,
Three fourteenths, pi, square root of two, and e:
Thus speak the men who count and measure stars
And atoms, forces, and the speed of light.

The unknown squared times a, plus once again
The unknown multiplied by b, plus c
Equated all to naught: thus speak the men
Who solve the riddles which the world propounds.

Function, rate of change, derivative
And integral, real axis, complex plane:
Thus speak the men who touch infinity
And calculate the end of endless steps.

And all these terms are fictions of the mind,
Or symbols, curved or straight, connected here
And severed there, on paper. But man's mind,
That gives them meaning, makes them yield the truth.

What truth? A kind of truth which does not tell
What two may be, so much as tell that two
And three are five; a kind of truth that says
In signs if so and so, then such and such;

A kind of truth which winds long chains of thought,
Each accurate and clear and logical,
Susceptible of proof from axioms,
Into single compact cables for man's use.

And with these cables of imagination,
Man binds a world together to his ends,
And manufactures riches. Mathematics,
Queen thou art of man's imagining.

Edmund C. Berkeley, 1944

160 VARIABLES IN OFFICE OPERATIONS

Accounts:
  Expenses
    materials
    labor
    services
    taxes
    shipping
    repairs
    rent

travel
postage
equipment
furniture
fixtures
buildings
transportation
Income
sales
services
rentals
interest
dividends
Other Items
overhead
gross profit
net profit
fixed assets
other assets
good will
liabilities
surplus
proprietorship
capital
Transactions
debit
credit
transfer
journal entry
ledger entry
cost of goods sold
cost of services sold
Cost Accounting
price
cost
margin
budget amount
depreciation
Customer Purchase Order:
customer identification
list of items on order
list of quantities on order
customer bill-to address
customer ship-to address
customer credit category
customer's authorization of order

customer's delivery requirements
warehouse picking instructions
Employee Attendance:
employee identification
day identification
on time and present
tardy but present
absent
present but left early
out on medical appointment
out on business
out for illness
Employee Classification:
employee identification
part time
full time
hourly
salaried
officer
non-officer
office
factory
temporary
permanent
on trial
not on trial
summer
all year
student
not student
Employee Status:
employee identification
active
retired
withdrawn
laid-off
on vacation
on military leave
on leave for personal reasons
on temporary disability
on permanent disability
Hours Worked Classification:
employee identification
time period identification
regular

overtime
double overtime
eligible for overtime pay
not eligible for overtime pay

Leave Days Accounting:
employee identification
time period identification
vacation days credited
vacation days taken
sick leave credited
sick leave taken

Number or Symbol Identification:
descriptive identification
numeric, whole number
numeric, dollars and cents
numeric, whole number and decimal
percent
positive
negative
zero
alphanumeric
alphabetical
literal
abbreviation
abbreviated
rounded
truncated
typewriter symbol
punctuation
symbolic
binary
decimal

Payables Accounting:
supplier identification
delivery verification
invoice preparation
invoice verification
invoice approval
schedule date of payment

Person or Organization Identification:
identification code
name
street address
city address
state address

zip code
post office box number
bill-to address
ship-to address
credit rating
delinquent or not
employee
customer
supplier
consultant
stockholder
director

Personnel Records:
employee identification
date of birth
date of employment
date of retirement
date of death
date of withdrawal
dates of starting on leaves
dates of returning from leaves

Receivables Accounting:
customer identification
transaction identification
invoice preparation
receipt of payment
disputed invoices
delinquent receivables
standard messages for customers

Salesman Supervision:
salesman identification
salesman territory
sales for month
quota for month
sales for year to date
commission formula
commissions for month
commissions for year to date
salesman training

Stock Classification:
stock identification
stock description
unit quantity
unit price
unit cost

unit margin
in stock
out of stock
on order
expected delivery date
out of production at the supplier
reorder point
reorder quantity
supplier(s)
standard messages to customer

233 CEMENT-WORDS OF MATHEMATICS

1. Place and position
   a. Locations: at, before, ahead of, behind, beyond, over, above, under, below, underneath, in, inside of, out of, outside of, on, off, against, touching, around, near, beside, next, opposite to, between, among
   b. Regions: top, bottom, left, right, front, back, center, side, edge, corner, end, middle, neighborhood, surrounding
   c. Directions: to, toward, from, up, down, along, across, through, into, out of, onto, forward, backward, sideways

2. Shape, Form, and Structure: flat, plane, round, circle, point, dot, line, curve, angle, fork, bend, square, space, spacing, ball, globe, ring, loop, oval, coil, hole, bump, bulge, knob, stick up, project, cover, crack, fold, knot, hanging, hollow, block, lump, chunk, solid, surface

3. Size and Magnitude: big, great, large, little, small, size, long, high, tall, deep, far, thick, fat, full, wide, short, low, shallow, near, thin, empty, narrow, length, height, depth, distance

4. Comparison and Degree: more, most, less, least, equal, unequal, enough, -er (as in "taller"), -est (as in "tallest"), great, greatest, than, as much as, as little as, not so much as

5. Indefinite Numbers and Measurements: few, several, little, much, many, some, a handful of, a lot of, a number of, a quantity of, a great deal of, -s (as in "cats", meaning more than one); also other endings for the plural; not very, fairly, rather, somewhat, partly, almost, nearly, very, entirely, altogether, quite

6. Definite Numbers: one, a, an, two, bi-, three, tri-, thir-, four, for-, five, fif-, six, seven, eight, nine, ten, -teen, -ty, eleven, twelve, dozen, twenty, score, hundred, thousand, million, billion, zero, no, none, naught, once, twice, half, third, quarter, plus, and (not all meanings), times, minus, less, -th (as in "sixth"), divided by

7. Order: first, second, third, next, last, -th (as in "sixth," meaning sixth in sequence), arrange, pattern, map, collect, scatter, one after another, in order, in sequence, one by one, two by two, even, uneven, together, scattered, hit or miss, spaced, diagram

8. Variation and Approximation: by and large, on the average, about, roughly, approximately, range over, depend on, vary with, various

14 VERY FAMOUS NUMBERS

These fourteen numbers are the chief numbers which over the course of tens of thousands of years have caused human beings to think, to ask themselves questions as a part of studying the external world, and to derive answers. The period of time over which the thinking occurred is certainly longer than 12,000 years and may be longer than 100,000 years. Actual archeological evidence of naming and identifying numbers and thinking about them is indirect, but is related to the interpretation of religious practices, music, art, ceremony, and other ancient elements of culture.

Number	Definition
0	zero, the quantity of nothing, recognized as a number by the Hindus and the Arabs long before it was recognized by the Romans and the Europeans; the start of the X axis of positive real numbers running to the right; the middle of the X X′ axis of positive and negative reals running to the right and the left
1	unity, one, recognized as a number before the dawn of history; the difference between "boy" and "boys," "thing" and "things"; the concept "singular" recorded in Greek and other languages
2	two, recognized as the number after one, and giving rise to the dual number in Greek and other languages; recognized as a number in prehistory
MANY	an indefinite number, with at least two meanings "more than one" and "more than two"; the concept "plural"; recognized as a number in prehistory
−1	the negative of one; minus one; one unit to the left from 0 (the origin, zero) on the X X′ axis of positive and negative real numbers; recognized as a number in the 1500's
i	the unit of imaginary numbers; the square root of minus one, $\sqrt{-1}$; the unit of measurement on the Y axis up and down (at a right angle) from the X axis; recognized as a number in the 1800's
1.4142...	the square root of 2, identified by the Pythagoreans about 300 BC as an incommensurable number (irrational number), a number that cannot be the quotient of one whole number by another whole number; the first irrational number recognized
2.7183...	the number called e, the sum of the exponential series $(1 + 1 + \frac{1}{2} + \frac{1}{6} + \frac{1}{24} + \frac{1}{120} ...)$; the base of "natural logarithms"; recognized in the 1500's as a profoundly important number in the computation of powers and logarithms
3.1416...	the number called pi or π; the ratio of a semicircle to its radius; recognized as a number by the Ancient Greeks; a subject of the Tennessee legislature at one time, when it passed a law that π should be equal to 3 and $\frac{1}{7}$ (3.1429...)
5	the number of fingers on one hand; in many languages the word "five" and the word "hand" are closely re-

85

lated; recognized in prehistory

10   the basis of the decimal system of notation of numbers; the number of fingers (digits) on two hands; the scale of notation invented by the Arabs (the Arabic numerals); also the basis of some forms of the abacus, a machine based on counters and locations on a board, or beads and strings on a frame; recognized as a number in prehistory

29 +   the number of earth days from one new moon to the next new moon, and basis of a calendar "moon-th"; recognized as a number in prehistory

365 +   the number of earth days from one vernal equinox to the next vernal equinox; the basis of the return of the seasons; the basis of the calendar year; recognized as a number in prehistory

∞   infinity, the limit of 1 divided by X as X becomes smaller and smaller and smaller approaching zero as a limit; a number that is greater than any given number; in a computer the largest number that that computer can represent in a storage location within that computer, such as 10 to the 63rd power times .9999999999; associated with some special provisions for overflow and stopping the program; used especially to prevent a computer trying to execute "infinite loops" such as "add 1 to the running total S"; recognized as a number in the 1600's

78 NUMBER WORDS AND THEIR RELATIVE FREQUENCY IN ENGLISH

a	117222
an	13897
one	17569
two	5958
three	2873
four	1637
five	1462
six	806
seven	615
eight	657
nine	468
ten	1260
eleven	227
twelve	413
thirteen	92
fourteen	143
fifteen	410
sixteen	194
seventeen	139
eighteen	215
nineteen	109
twenty	673
thirty	341
forty	283
fifty	525
sixty	161
seventy	59
seventy-five	61
eighty	82
ninety	62
hundred	1355
thousand	1240
million	598
billion	93
trillion	0
milliard	0
myriad	26

dozen	494	several	827
score	219	figure	1202
infinity	5	once	2957
none	601	twice	402
no	11742	thrice	7
first	5154	twain	18
half	1984	zero	50
second	926		

(Source: compiled from the *Lorge Magazine* count of 4 and ½ million words of English text, reported in *The Teacher's Word Book of 30,000 Words,* by Edward L. Thorndike and Irving Lorge, published by the Bureau of Publications of Teachers College, Columbia Univ., New York, 1944)

third	501
fourth	221
fifth	193
sixth	65
quarter	399
seventh	59
couple	577
pair	374
triple	18
quadruple	4
quintuple	0
halves	40
halve	14
both	1703
some	5761
any	6532
all	17799
few	2740
last	3517
least	1259
many	3874
more	8015
most	3443
less	1357
much	4816
number	954

COMPUTER SPACE REQUIRED TO STORE ONE MILLION CHARACTERS OF INFORMATION

Year	Cubic Feet
1953	400
1959	100
1971	8
1976	0.3
1981	0.03

(Source: reprinted with permission from *U.S. News & World Report,* April 20, 1981 issue, Copyright 1981, U.S. News & World Report, Inc.)

26 DECIMAL NUMBERS CONVERTED FROM DECIMAL TO HEXADECIMAL, OCTAL AND BINARY NOTATION

Decimal	Hexadecimal	Octal	Binary
0	0	0	0
1	1	1	1

2	2	2	10
3	3	3	11
4	4	4	100
5	5	5	101
6	6	6	110
7	7	7	111
8	8	10	1000
9	9	11	1001
10	A	12	1010
11	B	13	1011
12	C	14	1100
13	D	15	1101
14	E	16	1110
15	F	17	1111
16	10	20	10,000
17	11	21	10,001
18	12	22	10,010
19	13	23	10,011
20	14	24	10,100
50	32	62	110,010
100	64	144	1,100,100
500	1F4	764	111,110,100
1,000	3E8	1750	1,111,101,000
5,000	1,388	11,610	1,001,110,001,000

BINARY ADDITION

+	0	1
0	0	1
1	1	10

BINARY MULTIPLICATION

×	0	1
0	0	0
1	0	1

OCTAL ADDITION

+	0	1	2	3	4	5	6	7
0	0	1	2	3	4	5	6	7
1	1	2	3	4	5	6	7	10
2	2	3	4	5	6	7	10	11
3	3	4	5	6	7	10	11	12
4	4	5	6	7	10	11	12	13
5	5	6	7	10	11	12	13	14
6	6	7	10	11	12	13	14	15
7	7	10	11	12	13	14	15	16

OCTAL MULTIPLICATION

x	0	1	2	3	4	5	6	7
0	0	0	0	0	0	0	0	0
1	0	1	2	3	4	5	6	7
2	0	2	4	6	10	12	14	16
3	0	3	6	11	14	17	22	25
4	0	4	10	14	20	24	30	34
5	0	5	12	17	24	31	36	43
6	0	6	14	22	30	36	44	52
7	0	7	16	25	34	43	52	61

HEXADECIMAL ADDITION

+	0	1	2	3	4	5	6	7	8	9	A	B	C	D	E	F
0	0	1	2	3	4	5	6	7	8	9	A	B	C	D	E	F
1	1	2	3	4	5	6	7	8	9	A	B	C	D	E	F	10
2	2	3	4	5	6	7	8	9	A	B	C	D	E	F	10	11
3	3	4	5	6	7	8	9	A	B	C	D	E	F	10	11	12
4	4	5	6	7	8	9	A	B	C	D	E	F	10	11	12	13
5	5	6	7	8	9	A	B	C	D	E	F	10	11	12	13	14
6	6	7	8	9	A	B	C	D	E	F	10	11	12	13	14	15
7	7	8	9	A	B	C	D	E	F	10	11	12	13	14	15	16
8	8	9	A	B	C	D	E	F	10	11	12	13	14	15	16	17
9	9	A	B	C	D	E	F	10	11	12	13	14	15	16	17	18
A	A	B	C	D	E	F	10	11	12	13	14	15	16	17	18	19
B	B	C	D	E	F	10	11	12	13	14	15	16	17	18	19	1A
C	C	D	E	F	10	11	12	13	14	15	16	17	18	19	1A	1B
D	D	E	F	10	11	12	13	14	15	16	17	18	19	1A	1B	1C
E	E	F	10	11	12	13	14	15	16	17	18	19	1A	1B	1C	1D
F	F	10	11	12	13	14	15	16	17	18	19	1A	1B	1C	1D	1E

HEXADECIMAL MULTIPLICATION

×	0	1	2	3	4	5	6	7	8	9	A	B	C	D	E	F
0	0	0	0	0	0	0	0	0	0	0	0	0	0	0	0	0
1	0	1	2	3	4	5	6	7	8	9	A	B	C	D	E	F
2	0	2	4	6	8	A	C	E	10	12	14	16	18	1A	1C	1E
3	0	3	6	9	C	F	12	15	18	1B	1E	21	24	27	2A	2D
4	0	4	8	C	10	14	18	1C	20	24	28	2C	30	34	38	3C
5	0	5	A	F	14	19	1E	23	28	2D	32	37	3C	41	46	4B
6	0	6	C	12	18	1E	24	2A	30	36	3C	42	48	4E	54	5A
7	0	7	E	15	1C	23	2A	31	38	3F	46	4D	54	5B	62	69
8	0	8	10	18	20	28	30	38	40	48	50	58	60	68	70	78
9	0	9	12	1B	24	2D	36	3F	48	51	5A	63	6C	75	7E	87
A	0	A	14	1E	28	32	3C	46	50	5A	64	6E	78	82	8C	96
B	0	B	16	21	2C	37	42	4D	58	63	6E	79	84	8F	9A	A5
C	0	C	18	24	30	3C	48	54	60	6C	78	84	90	9C	A8	B4
D	0	D	1A	27	34	41	4E	5B	68	75	82	8F	9C	A9	B6	C3
E	0	E	1C	2A	38	46	54	62	70	7E	8C	9A	A8	B6	C4	D2
F	0	F	1E	2D	3C	4B	5A	69	78	87	96	A5	B4	C3	D2	E1

11 PROBLEMS IN ARITHMETIC FOR SUPPLE MINDS

The Dog on the Manakin Road / On the Manakin Road lives a Dog who barks for forty minutes every night whenever someone goes by at night. What is the smallest number of passers by that will keep him barking all night? Allow 10 and ½ hours.

Ignatius Trott's Conscience / Ignatius Trott, had at the age of 7 years a Conscience able to support a weight of 22 pounds. The weight it could carry increased every year thereafter 16 pounds. What weight can his Conscience support at his present age, 47 and ½ years?

Rabbit Hunting / Mr. Thompson of Yell County, aged 51, and his Dog, aged 2 years and 4 months, can get one Rabbit in eight hours' hunting. How many could they catch in the months November, December, January, and February? Allow 12 hours for a day's hunting, and deduct Sundays.

Eating Watermelons / A Boy and his Sister, ages 7 and 8, are eating Watermelons. Working jointly, it takes them 5 minutes to consume the first Melon, 10 minutes the second, 15 minutes the third, etc., etc. What will be the number of the Watermelon which will require 1 hour and 35 minutes for its consumption?

Cutting Teeth / Mr. and Mrs. Teddy Robinson, who live 17 and ½ miles north of Bumpusburg, say that their Baby, aged 7 months, cuts regularly 2 Teeth per month. At this rate, how many Teeth should he cut in 2 years and 3 months?

An Investment in Gum-Drops / Three

Boys, Jacob, aged 12, Harry, aged 9, and Alpheus, aged 7, have money to spend at the store. Jacob suggests that they buy Gum-Drops and they do so. Alpheus contributes 30¢, Harry 10¢, and Jacob 5¢. Harry consumes the Gum-Drops twice as fast as Alpheus, and Jacob 1 and ½ times as fast as Harry. How many cents' worth does each Boy eat? What was each Boy's gain or loss on the investment?

Opossum Eating Persimmons / An Opossum intends to eat three Persimmons every other half hour during nights of 11 and ½ hours. Being weak in Arithmetic, he makes an error, and eats four Persimmons every other 20 minutes of the time indicated. If each Persimmon gives him 1 and ½ pleasure-pounds, how much does he gain or lose from his deficiency in Arithmetic during the month of October?

The Beautiful Kitten Sennacherib / A beautiful Kitten Sennacherib, aged 2 months and 3 weeks, caught the mange (a word derived from the French manger, to eat — always seize every chance to acquire useful information) from having been too much played with and petted by the children. If before catching the mange, she possessed 17,660 hairs, and lost 218 hairs a day, how many did she have left after 81 days?

Reading the *Trail of the Lonesome Pine* / Mrs. Cornwallis Dabney, age unknown, of Porpoise Center, while rocking to sleep her Baby, aged 19 months, named Bogardus, read 231 pages of Fox's *Trail of the Lonesome Pine*. Continuing reading at the same rate, she read the remaining 191 pages in 2 hours and 10 minutes, while pitting 3 quarts of cherries. At the same rate, how long would it take her to pit 5 gallons of cherries? How long did it take her to put Bogardus to sleep?

Boy Eating Pancakes / If a Boy can eat 5 Pancakes in 1 minute by using both hands, how many can he eat in 1 hour and 29 minutes?

An Old White Cow, aged 14, had been sold by a stingy Farmer, and was being led away, tied to a heavy wagon. The Farmer sold her because she was old, and because he might never again be offered $36 for her. She had no name; except the one which her pretty little Calf, aged 2 months and 3 weeks, gave her, and that was Mah. She wanted to remain with her Baby, and she pulled back all she could on the rope about her horns, and lowed constantly to her darling, who ran along the fence. Soon the little Calf could see her Mama no longer, but her little ears could hear her Mama for ¾ mile plus 22 feet, and you can figure what that distance was. But her Mama could hear just twice as far, and then, so great was the love of her mother-heart, that by hardly breathing, she heard her Baby for 200 yards further, and you can figure how many feet this was. Then the night wind came out of the forest, and the sound of the leaves drowned everything, and she never heard her child's voice again. If you multiply the number of feet she had walked up to this time by the infinite number of things she had passed and was to pass — the fence-posts, the blades of grass by the road, the leaves on the trees, the pebbles, the grains of sand, the stars in the sky — you will have something approaching the number of sorrows which pressed upon her old heart.

(Source: *The Boys' Own Arithmetic* by Raymond Weeks, E.P. Dutton & Co., New York, 1924, 188 pp)

6 PROPERTIES OF PRIME NUMBERS

Definition: A prime number is a whole number which is exactly divisible only by itself and one.

Examples: The first ten prime numbers are 1, 2, 3, 5, 7, 11, 13, 17, 19, 23.

Theorem: There is no largest prime (contained in Euclid's *Elements*: proved.)

Problem: Given the ordinal number n (such as 10) of the prime p (such as 23), compute the prime by a formula using n. / No one has ever done this.

Procedure for Computing Primes: Write out all the numbers in sequence up to n. Cross out all the multiples of primes less than the square root of n. The numbers that are left are the primes. / With some minor improvements over 2000 years, this remains the only effective method for finding all primes up to n.

Conjecture: Any even number n can be expressed as the sum of two primes. / This conjecture was stated in a letter by the mathematician Goldbach in 1742. It is undoubtedly true, and the number of "Goldbach pairs" (which is three for the even number 22, namely 11 and 11, 5 and 17, 3 and 19) approaches infinity as the even number n increases, but an acceptable "mathematical" proof has never been found.

12 CLASSES THAT HAVE NO MEMBERS AT ALL

Odd numbers that are divisible by 2

Circles that are square

Fire-breathing dragons

Unicorns

Apples that are all red and all green

Barbers who always shave themselves and never shave themselves

Perpetual motion machines

Former species of animals that have become extinct, such as the dodo and the passenger pigeon, probably the woolly mammoth, and certainly the giant sloth and tyrannosaurus

Perfect squares (such as 9, 16, 25 ...) whose last digit (in the decimal notation) is 2, 3, 7 or 8

Persons who can eat 200 large apple pies in one day

Angels with large white wings and golden halos

Devils with cloven hoofs and forked tails

12 CLASSES THAT HAVE AT LEAST A BILLION BILLION MEMBERS (10 to the 18th power)

Atoms

Leaves of plants and trees

Grains of quartz sand

Snowflakes

Numbers 1, 2, 3, 4, 5 and so on

Thousandths of a second elapsed since the Earth began

Drops of water in the ocean

Stars in all the galaxies

Kilometers across our Galaxy

Electrons

Living cells

Number of possible curves that could be drawn on one letter-size sheet of paper

30 PRINCIPLES FOR SOLVING PROBLEMS

The Principle of Ignorance:
"What you don't know won't hurt you"

The Principle of Fate:
"Allah wills it"

The Principle of Waiting:
"Everything comes to him who waits"

The Principle of Postponement:
"Never do today what you can put off till tomorrow"

The Principle of Procrastination:
"If you wait long enough, the problem will take care of itself"

The Principle of Mr. Micawber:
"Something will turn up"
(He was a character in *David Copperfield* by Charles Dickens, published 1850)

The Principle of Pure Chance:
"Let's flip a coin"

The Principle of Nonsense:
"Let's see what the horoscope indicates"

The Principle of Denial:
"There is really no problem at all — you're just worrying over nothing"

The Principle of Intuition:
"Let your subconscious work on it while you sleep"

The Principle of Willpower:
"Man has free will and can choose or not choose"

The Principle of Tolerance:
"De gustibus non disputandum" — "about tastes there is no sense in disputing"

The Principle of Forgiveness:
"Forgive them, for they know not what they do"

The Principle of Departure:
"That problem is not for me, and I am leaving"

The Principle for dealing with Mountains:
"If the mountain won't come to Mahomet, Mahomet must go to the mountain"

The Principle of Faultfinding:
"It's your fault it does not work"

The Principle of Poor Me:
"Nothing ever goes right for me"

The Principle of Excuse:
"This is why it did not work — listen ..."

The Principle of Not Invented Here:
"Any method or idea not invented here is no good"

The Principle of Action:
"Don't just stand there — do something, anything"

The Principle of Authority:
"Consult an expert, and do what he says"

The Principle of Experience:
"Experience is the best teacher"

The Principle of Trial and Error:
"If at first you don't succeed, try and try again"

The Principle of Successive Approximation:
"If at first you don't succeed, try some more — but learn from each trial"

The Principle of Theory and Practice:
"Theory enriches practice, and practice modifies theory"

The Principles of Calculation:
"Figure it out, compute it"

The Principle of Feedback Control:
"Every time the process strays off a little, correct it, bring it back to the desired condition"

The Principles of Science and the Scientific Method:
"Experiment, draw conclusions, and test them"

The Principles of Systems Analysis and Synthesis:

"Take all the factors into account"

The Principle of Careful, Systematic Verification:

"Continually check all statements — they tend to get out of date"

(Source: editorial by E.C. Berkeley, published in *Computers and Automation*, March, 1973)

27 PRINCIPLES FOR SOLVING PROBLEMS IN OFFICE OPERATIONS

The Principle of Precedent

"If there is a precedent, use it"

The Principle of Higher Authority

"Ask the boss, and do what he says"

The Principle of Consulting

"Consult an expert, and apply his advice"

The Principle of Noninvolvement

"That problem is none of our business — let's not get involved"

The Principle of the Committee

"Since the problem affects several areas of the company, let's appoint a committee to reach a consensus"

The Principle of the Commission

"Since the problem calls for more understanding, let's appoint a commission to investigate for several months and make recommendations"

The Principle of No Innovation

"Since the solution to the problem smacks of something new and unproved, let's have nothing to do with it"

The Principle of Not Invented Here

"Since the solution to the problem was not invented here, let's have nothing to do with it"

The Principle of No Solution

"Since the problem, after much effort spent, has no apparent solution, we must accept that"

The Principle of Denial

"If the problem is looked at in the right way, there is no problem at all"

The Principle of Delay

"Let's delay for a while, because something might turn up"

The Principle of Indefinite Procrastination

"If we delay long enough, the problem should evaporate and disappear"

The Principle of Experience

"See what experience we have had on the problem, and do what experience indicates"

The Principle of Minimum Expense

"See what solution will cost the least, and choose that one"

The Principle of Maximum Profit

"See what solution will yield the most profit, and choose that one"

The Principle of Least Trouble

"See what solution will produce the least trouble, and choose that one"

The Principle of "the Customer is Always Right"

"See what solution will make the customer the most satisfied, and choose that one"

The Principle of "the Squeaking Wheel"

"See what solution will stop the biggest squeak, and choose that"

The Principle of "Reinventing the Wheel"

"Since it is too much bother to search out the best prior solution, let's reinvent a new best solution"

The Principle of Trial and Error

"If at first we don't succeed, let's try and try again"

The Principle of Successive Approximation

"If at first we don't succeed, let's try and

try again, but learn what not to do from each trial"

The Principle of Systematic Analysis and System Synthesis
"Take all factors and variables into account; then build and test the system until it works well"

The Principle of Successive Cases from Simple to Complex
"Solve the problem first for a simple case; then solve it for successively more complicated cases"

The Principle of Feedback Control
"Every time the process strays off a little, correct it, bring it back to the desired condition"

The Principle of Calculation
"Figure it out, compute it"

The Principle of the Scientific Method
"Experiment, draw conclusions, test them — repeat until satisfactory"

The Principle of Continuing Verification
"Continually check all statements and conditions — everything always gets out of date"

43 PRINCIPLES OF STRATEGY IN CHESS

Play
Use all your pieces.
Accumulate small advantages — in position, mobility, development, etc.
Prefer lasting advantages to temporary ones.
Before deciding on a move to accomplish something, see what other moves will do the same thing.
In a tournament, if you see a good move, look five minutes for a better one.
Make sure you use every move to best advantage.

Place your pieces if possible where they cannot be disturbed or removed.
Don't make a move which your opponent can force you to retract.

Development:
Develop first; attack afterwards.
Bring all your pieces to bear.
Develop rooks.
In the opening, move no piece more than once, if possible.
In the opening, make no more than two pawn moves.
Strive to control the center of the board.

Attack:
Always play with a definite imagined position in view in which you exert maximum force against your opponent.
Attack only if based on a better position and a heavier force.
Aim to effectively isolate the king.
To win a piece, the number of attacks must be one more than the number of protections.
Don't attack with insufficient forces.
Make a serious attack only with at least four pieces working together.
A system of alternating attacks upon two or more weaknesses tends to cramp and disrupt your opponent's position.
Seek to win a pinned piece by multiplying the number of attacks.
A superior attack may be a sufficiently good defense.

Defense:
Make your side hang together — the pieces protecting each other — so that if pressure develops, you have a first line of defense.
Watch out for; simultaneous attacks, unprotected pieces, uncovered attacks, uncovered check.
Beware of bait.
Strategically important points should be overprotected.

Exchange:

Exchange: to gain tempo, to avoid retreat, to avoid time-wasting defensive moves, to simplify when your forces are superior, to seize an open file, or to force your opponent out of a strong position.

Don't exchange without good reason, since your pieces should be well placed.

If you are behind, don't exchange and don't let your opponent exchange.

Mobility:

Of two moves otherwise equal, choose the one giving the greater mobility.

Limiting the choice of moves of your opponent is a considerable advantage, especially when repeated several times in succession.

Blocking an opponent's piece is almost as good as taking it.

Seize an open file, and use it to advance to the seventh or eighth rank.

Two bishops raking adjacent long diagonals exert great force.

Pawns:

The plus of a pawn can win a game.

An opponent's pawns may be a most valuable barrier to his attack.

Isolate your opponent's pawns — to take them, and to post your pieces in front.

Aim for a majority of pawns on the queen's side for the end game.

A good configuration of pawns tends to be a lasting advantage.

Knowledge:

Know winning positions to reach.

Book knowledge is most necessary in the ending.

The most important study in chess is thorough analysis of masters' games.

(Source: *Strategy in Chess* by Edmund C. Berkeley, published by Berkeley Enterprises Inc., New York, NY, 1952)

11 Computers and Logic, Boolean Algebra, Fallacies, . . .

THE USE OF LOGIC, AND THE SMELL OF SMOKE

People are more familiar with numbers than they are with logic, although they use logic all the time without thinking about it. Numbers show up in one of the first operations dealing with intellectual ideas taught all over the world to young people — counting: one, two, three, four ... ten, eleven, twelve ... one hundred, one hundred and one, ..., one thousand, ...

Logic shows up in the use of words like "IF, NO, THE, OF, IS, NOT, YES, NO, AND, OR...." The use of these words is absorbed by young children out of everyday experience, talking, and listening, and begins with the earliest words used between the child and its close family. Practice with these words starts usually about age 1 and ¼, and continues to the age of reflection, and beyond. For a few people the age of reflection begins about age 8, and for other people, about ages 16, 20, or 30. At the age of reflection, young people start wondering about how all that surrounds them fits together into a sensible or reasonable pattern, which may be called a "world-view." A young person I once knew, at age 7 and ½ came on Christmas Day into the room full of presents prepared by his family, and after looking around, he announced, "Well, there are two things I don't understand — how Santa Claus comes down the chimney and how babies come into the world."

One item for reflection is the meaning of "IF," and how one can express that idea in other ways, such as "SUPPOSE, IN CASE, IN THE EVENT THAT."

An example of everyday use of logic comes from smelling smoke. Suppose you notice the smell of smoke. At once you start looking over your situation to decide what you will do — because "If I smell smoke, there may be danger." You sniff the room, the corridor. Then you put your head outdoors, and sniff. There is a much stronger smell. You check on the wind direction, you listen for any fire alarms, and so on. Suppose the time is autumn, and the place northern California. You say to yourself, "Probably farmers are burning off the rice stubble, and somebody is watching." You hear no fire alarms. "Must be all right. I can go back to what I am doing." Logic, plus observation, solves your problem.

There is here no issue of mathematics, or discussion, or language, or science, beyond common knowledge. But there is an issue of logic and of reasoning, springing from an IF sentence, a condition.

Another important reason why logic is not noticed is because very often a person can say something to somebody else without being very careful about what he is saying — without being accurate in the expression of his ideas. Nearly always the situation is so concrete that only a tiny amount of expression is needed to answer or respond to a question, because the situation conveys all the other information.

But the advance of personal computers is producing an increased interest and attention to logic, especially with respect to programming and algorithms.

15 STATEMENTS THAT ARE BEYOND CONTRADICTION

What was was.

What is is.

What will be will be.

What must be must be.

Anything is itself.

The birth and death of a man happen only once in his lifetime.

Things are more like what they are now than they have ever been before. — Dwight D. Eisenhower.

The game is not over until it is over. — Yogi Berra

Needs must when the devil drives.

A is A.

If A is A, then it is undeniable that A is A.

A rose is a rose is a rose. — Gertrude Stein

Half of infinity is equal to infinity.

Half of zero is equal to zero.

For any finite number N that you can name, there is another number that is bigger, such as N plus one.

7 SUBJECTS WHICH ARE THE MAIN CONTENT OF SYMBOLIC LOGIC

Subject	Example of Content
statements, sentences, propositions	x has the property P John has a computer

truth, falsity, assertion, denial	yes, no on, off true, false 1, 0
reasoning, implications, theorems, proofs	If S then T, and if T then U IMPLIES if S then U. If Andover beats Exeter, and if Exeter beats Plymouth, then Andover beats Plymouth
individuals, elements, things	x, y, z, . . . x, x sub one, x sub 2, . . . x, x prime, x second, . . . x, another x, a third x, . . .
properties	that x has the property P that John has a computer
relations	that x has the relation R to y that John is a parent of Max that St. Louis is between New York and Los Angeles
classes, groups, collections, sets	K, a class x, a member x member K, x is in K, x is a member of K compass directions, a class N, E, S, W are compass directions
choosing, selecting, arranging, comparing, matching, merging, collating, sorting, sequencing, ordering, permuting,...	sort T E A in alphabetic sequence

6 COMPARISONS OF MATHEMATICS AND SYMBOLIC LOGIC

Mathematics	Symbolic Logic
Deals with numbers like 3, ⅖, .417	Deals with classes like switches, gates, contacts
Deals with shapes like circle, square, curve	Deals with relations like between, imply, deduction
Deals with patterns like those in a tiled floor	Deals with proofs, induction, consequences
Answers questions like: how much? how many? how far? how often?	Answers questions like: is this true? what does this mean? are there any loopholes?

Has operations like PLUS, MINUS, TIMES, DIVIDED BY, APPROACHES, DERIVATIVE	Has operations like AND, OR, NOT, FOR EVERY, FOR NO, IF, EXCEPT
Numbers cannot be handled by computers without mathematical ideas	Conditions, decisions, programming, cannot be handled by computers without the ideas of symbolic logic

3 SAMPLE STATEMENTS OF SYMBOLIC LOGIC

To make clear specific ideas of symbolic logic, and show how they apply, we shall choose an illustrative context, which is not mathematical, and which belongs in the common everyday experience of all people: the context of family relationships. Within this context we can show how these relationships can be described using two kinds of words: words which belong specifically to the field of family relationships (we can call them "brick" words); and words which are completely general and belong in symbolic logic (we can call them "cement" words).

Problem 1: Define *father* in terms of *parent* and *male*, and separate between the brick words and cement words.

Solution: Definition: A *person* is the *father* of another *person* if and only if he is *male* and is the *parent* of that other *person*.

Separating the two kinds of words, we have:

(a) Words which belong in the field of family relationships (brick words): *person, father, male, parent;*
(b) Words which belong in the field of symbolic logic (cement words): A .... is the .... of another .... if and only if it (we replace "he" by "it" to avoid the idea of animateness) is .... and is the .... of that other .... .

Problem 2: Express *uncle* in terms of *parent* and *male*.
Solution: First, we shall define *brother*.

Definition: A *person* is a *brother* of another *person* if and only if he is *male* and there is some *person* who is *parent* of both of them.

Brick words (words which belong to family relationships): *person, brother, male, parent.*

Cement words (words which belong to symbolic logic): A .... is a .... of another .... if and only if it is .... and there is some .... which is a .... of both of them. (We must change "who" to "which" so as not to imply animateness.)

Second, having defined *brother* let us define *uncle*

Definition: A *person* is an *uncle* of another *person* if and only if he is a *brother* of a *parent* of that other *person*.

Brick words: *person, uncle, male, brother, parent.*

Cement words: A .... is a .... of another .... if and only if it is a .... of a .... of that other .... .

Now, we need to get rid of some of the shapelessness of these patterns of logical words, because of their blanks. We need to take out the blanks and put in the most general ideas that are implied by the blanks.

To help us in this process, and enable us to imagine the ideas a little better, let us use "thing" instead of "person". (Actually "entity" or "element" or "individual" would be better words, in the sense of being more technically correct, because we intend to designate non-physical things also; but "thing" is a comfortable everyday kind of word, and is not an unreasonable choice.)

Also, let us use capital letters F, M, P, B, U to take the place of words *father, male, parent, brother, uncle.*

With these changes, our three statements become:

Statement 1: A thing is the F of another thing if and only if it (the first-mentioned thing) is M, and is a P of that other thing (the second-mentioned thing).

Statement 2: A thing is a B of another thing if and only if it is M and there exists something which is a P of both of them.

Statement 3: A thing is a U of another thing if and only if it is a B of a P of that other thing.

THE CONCEPT OF A CLASS

The concept of a class, group, kind, sort, type, collection, or species is an extremely fundamental idea — fundamental in the same way that the idea of a statement (or proposition or assertion) is fundamental — one of the foundation stones of thought.

The idea of a class, of course, comes from observations of the real world, the scientific world. I can think of no better comment on the idea of class as derived from observations of the real world than the following remarks made about thirty years ago by Sir George Paget Thomson, a well-known physicist and Nobel prize winner:

There is one feature of the world we live in which is so general and so universal that it seems to have escaped proper notice. For want of a better name, I will call it the "principle of mass production". It is the tendency which nature shows to repeat almost indefinitely each entity it makes. This is most obvious perhaps among the smallest of objects. There are about enough atoms in the ink that makes one letter of this sentence to provide one not only for every inhabitant of the earth, but one for every creature if each star of our galaxy had a planet as populous as the earth. But there are in the universe less than one hundred kinds of atoms, and these hundred themselves are made of a very small number, two or three, of common constituents; electrons, protons, and neutrons (if the latter are to be given independent status). At this level the individuals of the multitude are identical; that they are strictly indistinguishable is a principle of the quantum theory which might rank with our other principles, ... Larger objects are no longer strictly identical but closely similar. Examples come both from animate and from inanimate nature. Drops of rain, grains of sand, particles of smoke, bacteria, the cells of any piece of apparently homogeneous organic tissue, in every case though there may be a large variety of distinguishable kinds, each kind exists in numbers which even the cold mathematician must describe as considerable and which to the ordinary person are incalculably immense.

Especially in the living world this is noticeable. A beech tree is one of a species which contains a vast number of individuals, each indeed different, but clearly distinguished from other creatures made of much the same materials — whales or orchids for example. Each tree has in season a large though perhaps not quite so large number of leaves; each leaf is made up of relatively few kinds of cell, each kind present in very large numbers.

To my mind this multitudinousness is the outstanding fact in the universe as we know it. There is nothing in logic to demand it. Though apparent to the careful observer using only his unaided senses, the advance of scientific instruments and knowledge makes it much more striking. To a certain extent indeed it is the result of language; we give names to recognizable classes and since we have only a limited number of names, the classification is sometimes arbitrary, giving the impression of sharply defined species where perhaps none exists. But it is more true to say that natural classification has moulded our language. Because there exist recognizable groups each containing many individuals, man has invented the "universals" which have played such a part in metaphysical argument.

This, one may be sure, is one of the fundamentals of the world which further discovery will not alter. Atomicity in its widest sense, mass production by nature, is the deepest of scientific truths.

ARE THERE OTHER IDEAS THAT MAY BE EXPRESSED IN EFFICIENT SYMBOLS?

After this look at the basic ideas of symbolic logic it is appropriate to ask several questions:

1. Are there other ideas in language that can be crystallized out into efficient symbols that can be calculated with?
2. Is there a possibility that all the language of thought can become calculable like mathematics and symbolic logic?
3. Is it conceivable that, in the future, arguments of all kinds will be settled not by human beings arguing about them but by automatic computers calculating the answers?

I believe that the answer to all of these questions is "yes."

Ordinary natural language is the matrix, the ore, the molten rock, out of which crystallize the diamond-like ideas and symbols of mathematics and symbolic logic. As human beings understand more and more the natural languages they use, the ways in which these languages reveal and hide ideas, and reflect and distort concepts, the more they will manage to extract from languages the crystals and nuggets of clarity that are to be found in such fields as mathematics and symbolic logic. The crucial point, of course, is not making a new symbol, but making useful symbols that can be calculated with and that can be rigorously connected with a host of other symbols in the relations of logic and mathematics.

The history of the development of mathematics and symbolic logic is a clear proof of these views. Ideas that have been unexpressed or badly expressed in language for centuries have gradually come out of language and have been deposited in the fabric of efficient symbols. And the advent of powerful automatic computers will tend to hasten the process, opening great new realms of thought to symbolic calculation.

BOOLEAN ALGEBRA: THE TECHNIQUE FOR MANIPULATING *AND, OR, NOT* AND CONDITIONS

A part of symbolic logic which has found many useful and unexpected applications is the technique for handling AND, OR, NOT, and conditions, called Boolean algebra.

Some of these applications have been in the field of rules, contracts, and agreements; for example, classifications of cases and the corresponding actions to be taken with regard to them. In this example, Boolean algebra applies in making sure that sets of statements have no conflicts and no loopholes. Here, the kind of Boolean algebra is the algebra of classes — a technique for symbolic calculating about classes or collections of cases, with the connectives AND, OR, NOT, EXCEPT, etc.

Most of the important applications of Boolean algebra have been in the field of switches, circuits, signals, controlling and computing — various aspects of the field of the design and construction of intelligent machines. Here, Boolean algebra is the algebra of "on-off" circuit elements — it provides a technique for symbolic calculating about combinations of elements of circuits that may be either on or off, conducting or not conducting, in one position or the other position, etc., combined with physical connections that express AND, OR, NOT, EXCEPT, etc.

How can Boolean algebra apply to two such diverse fields? The reason is essentially that this algebra handles the ideas expressed in many of the commonest words of language. So it is reasonable to expect that Boolean algebra will apply in many fields, because these words are used in many fields.

One way to gain an idea of the content of Boolean algebra is to notice the words of ordinary language that are in the territory of Boolean algebra, in the same way that PLUS, MINUS, TIMES, DIVIDED BY are in the territory of ordinary algebra. But not all the meanings apply to Boolean algebra, since words are products of the evolution of language, and a word often has meanings from different territories of thought fused together within it. "But" and "and," when connecting two statements, are translated indistinguishably in Boolean algebra as AND, because they connect two statements to assert that they are both true. In other words, "but" has the same logical meaning of association as the word "and"; however, as compared with "and", "but" conveys an additional idea, "you would not have expected it", "contrary to expectation". And variations of expectation, expressed by the speaker to the listener, are not relevant in Boolean algebra.

62 COMMON WORDS AND PHRASES BELONGING TO BOOLEAN ALGEBRA

a
all
an
and
and/or
any
anything
are

be
both
but
class
collection
consists of
contains
each
either
either . . . or
empty
everything
except

excludes
excluding
group (meaning "class")
if
if and only if
if . . . , then
in
includes
including
is
is contained in
is included in
kind (meaning "class")
lies in
neither
neither . . . nor
no
none
nor
not
not both

nothing
only
only if
overlaps
or
or . . . or both
or . . . or . . . or any one or more of them
or . . . but not both
or else
overlaps
. . . s (meaning "plural")
set (meaning "class")
sort (meaning "class")
some
something
type (meaning "class")
unless
which is
which are
yes

14 FUNDAMENTAL CONCEPTS OF BOOLEAN ALGEBRA

The following is a set of postulates (or conditions or demands or specifications or requirements) defining Boolean algebra. This set was devised by Professor E.V. Huntington of Harvard University in 1904. Any mathematical system (or structure) that is truthfully described by these postulates is a Boolean algebra. There are many such systems or structures.

Concepts accepted as given:

a, b, c, ...   Elements; which may be thought of as items in a list K (possibly an infinite list)

OP (pronounced "opp")   An operation; which may be thought of as a rule by means of which any two items in the list, such as a and b, determine another item or items (maybe in this list, maybe not), collectively called a OP b. The rule in its essence is a two-way table showing for every value of a along the side and for every value of b along the top what item or items a OP b is or are. This operation is often designated + and sometimes designated v and sometimes designated in other ways.

Propositions accepted as given:

1. a OP a = a.
2. a OP b = b OP a.
3. (a OP b) OP c = a OP (b OP c).
4. There is at least one element z such that a OP z = a for every a.
5. There exists at least one element u such that u OP a = u for every a.
6. a OP b determines an element in K.
7. There exists at least one element a' for every a such that: if x OP a = a, and if x OP a' = a', then x = z (where z is an element such that b OP z = b for every b) and a OP a' = u (where u is an element such that u OP c = u for every c).
8. If a OP b is not equal to b, there exists at least one element x such that a OP x = a and b OP x = b and yet for some c, c OP x is not equal to c.

Definitions:

1. a IM b is equivalent to a OP b = b. IM is a relation. Often this relation is designated ⊂ and is pronounced "implies" or "lies in".
2. a AN b = (a' OP b')'. AN is another operation. Often this operation is designated · (a centered dot) and pronounced "and". Often this operation (like "times" in elementary algebra) is designated simply by adjacency (writing next to).
3. u, which turns out to be unique, since it can be quite easily proved from the postulates that there is only one u satisfying the postulates.
4. z, which turns out to be unique, since it can likewise be easily proved that there is only one z satisfying the postulates.

In other words, if we come across a collection or list of mathematical elements (which, of course, can be called a, b, c ....) and an operation (which of course can be called OP), which associates two of them and gives a third (which may or may not be the same), then we can find out, by testing the behavior of this mathematical system (i.e., collection and operation) against each of the foregoing eight statements, whether or not this system is a Boolean algebra.

7 INTERPRETATIONS OF THE POSTULATES OF BOOLEAN ALGEBRA

	Classes
a v b	a or b or both
ab	a and b
a'	not a

1	the universe class, u
0	the null class, z

On-Off Circuit Elements

a v b	a and b in parallel
ab	a and b in series
a'	current in a' when no current in a
1	current always, u
0	current never, z

Regions

a v b   the JOIN of a and b
ab   the UNION of a and b
a′   the region outside of a
1   everywhere, u
0   nowhere, z

Propositions

P v Q   P or Q or both
P·Q   both P and Q
~P   not-P
u   tautology, u
z   contradiction, z

Truth Values of Propositions

p v q   p v q
p·q   p·q
p′   p′
1   certainty, u

0   impossibility, z

Algebra of Two Numbers
1 and 0

p v q   p $+$ q $-$ pq
pq   pq
p′   1 $-$ p
1   1
0   0

Factors of 30

(1, 2, 3, 5, 6, 10, 15, 30) and factors of certain other numbers such as 66, 210,...

a v b   least common multiple of a and b
ab   greatest common divisor of a and b
a′   complement of a, quotient of a divided into 30
1   30
0   1

20 FORMULAS FOR TRUTH VALUE COMPUTATION BY COMPUTER

Truth Value	Computation
T (P OR Q)	$p + q - pq$

(The truth value of proposition P or proposition Q or both is p (the truth value of P) plus q (the truth value of Q) minus p times q. The truth value of a true proposition is 1, and the truth value of a false proposition is 0.)

T (P AND Q)	p·q, pq
T (NOT-P)	$1 - p$
T (P OR ELSE Q)	$p + q - 2pq$
T (P OR NOT-Q)	$1 - q + pq$
T (NOT-P OR Q)	$1 - p + pq$
T (P IF AND ONLY IF Q)	$1 - p - q + 2pq$
T (P IS TRUE)	p
T (P IS FALSE)	$1 - p$
T (P IS FALSE OR Q IS TRUE)	$1 - p + pq$
T (ANY TRUE PROPOSITION)	1
T (ANY FALSE PROPOSITION)	0
T (p = q)	$1 - p - q + 2pq$
T (p IS NOT EQUAL TO q)	$p + q - 2\ pq$
T (p IS GREATER THAN q)	$p - pq$
T (IF P, THEN Q)	$1 - p + pq$
T (SUPPOSE P, THEN Q)	$1 - p + pq$
T (IN THE EVENT P, THEN Q)	$1 - p + pq$
T (THE TRUTH VALUE OF P EQUALS THE TRUTH VALUE OF Q)	$1 - p - q + 2\ pq$

T (P IS THE SAME AS Q) is not determinate from p and q; instead P and Q have to be analyzed into subjects x and x′ and predicates S and S′; if the subjects x and x′ denote the same thing and the predicates S and S′ denote the same property, then
1. P is interchangeable with Q
2. P and Q have the same meaning
3. p = q
For example, P might be "the computer is failing" and Q might be "our computer is not working properly"; then p = q.

172 CEMENT WORDS OF LOGIC

1. Reports on Statements, Truth Values: yes, true, right, no, false, not so, wrong, truth, falsehood
2. Connectives of Statements or Terms: and, or, not, if ... then, if and only if, or else, and/or, except, unless, with, without, in other words, that is, namely, provided, suppose, let, assuming, also, together with, neither ... nor, nor, therefore
3. Name, Meaning: name, label, meaning, idea, be called, be named, stand for, mean, definition
4. Assertion: be, is, are, am, have, has, do, exist, happen, occur
5. Properties, Classes, Abstractions: kind, sort, type, class, example, instance, member, -ment (as in "employment"), -th (as in "width"), -dom (as in "freedom"), -ness (as in "sweetness"), -ty (as in "virility")
6. Relation Connectives: of, to, for, by, with, from, in, as to, in regard to, about, covering, in relation to, -ee (as in "employee"), -er (as in "employer"), -or (as in "visitor")
7. Variables: I, me, you, he, she, it, they, them, we, us, such as, which, who, this, these, that, those, do (as in "Do you ...?", "I do."), so (as in "I'll do so."), to (as in "I'd like to."), thing, body, person, one, A,B,C ... (as in "A buys a car, and sells it to B"), the former, the latter, John Doe, Richard Roe ...
8. Operators on Variables: all, each, every, both, either, any, not all, some, a, an, at least one, one, none, no, not any, neither, the
9. The Relation of Equal or Unequal: same as, equal to, identical with, different from, unequal to, other than
10. The Relation of Like or Unlike: like, unlike, similar to, dissimilar to
11. The Relation of Membership or Inclusion: in, part of, piece of, bit of, subdivision of, included in, excluded from, outside of
12. The Rest or Remainder: and so forth, and so on, etc., and the rest
13. Miscellaneous Properties and Relations: conflicting with, contradiction, consistent with, inconsistent with, overlapping with, correlated with, corresponding to, matching with, pairing with, gaps, loopholes, incomplete, complete, symmetric with, assymetric to, essence of, gist of, core of, kernel of, essentially, substantially, basically

LOGIC, DISTORTION, AND FALLACIES

We intend that a computer should behave logically. In other words, a computer should perform its operations to fit logically into the realities of a situation.

This is difficult. Realities have to be observed either by instruments or by human beings or both, and then they have to be interpreted into a language that a computer can understand. Then that language has to be input into the computer, and then the computer has to behave appropriately. The way the computer is to behave appropriately often requires another set of actions by instruments or human beings (or both) in expressing the program (or software) by means of which it is expected to behave appropriately.

The situation is often made muddier. The cause of the "mud" may be accidental or intentional, or "as if" it were intentional, because in this world we are dealing with animate organisms as well as inanimate things or processes. Here are some examples:

The octopus squirts an inky fluid to confuse and baffle its enemies.

The advertiser, the public relations expert, deliberately produces one-sided messages, fogs of words and pictures.

A certain fly seems just like a big wasp, with black and yellow striped body and wasp-like buzzing, but on closer attention it is not a wasp.

The term "disinformation" comes from the practice of government intelligence agencies to spread false information (lies), in order to confuse, mislead, and deny.

Establishments deliberately make life hell for whistle-blowers, for persons who tell tales, report facts that tarnish images and reputations.

Only the above-mentioned fly has no personal individual responsibility, for its spreading of disinformation. That behavior arises from its genes and its evolution.

Following is a collection of eight lists of fallacies. These are types of reasoning, which are wrong, invalid, and do not prove what they pretend to prove. Many of them have names that commemorate their use dating from the times of ancient Greece and Rome, more than 2000 years ago.

But these fallacies were not interesting to the creators and inventors of symbolic logic, such as George Boole, Lewis Carroll, and John Venn, for example, as they came across them in old textbooks of formal logic. So what did they do? They paid no attention to them, they ignored them. Why? Perhaps the principle used by a scholar, academician, or professor is: "If X does not fit into the exciting new territory I am working on, ignore X, forget X."

I have not found in the literature a good discussion of how certain statements that are fallacious when asserted in one instance can change very gradually into a reasonable statistical argument as the number of instances increases. For example, take the proposition "The sun will rise tomorrow." No quantity of positive instances can prove that this statement is universally true. Based on the history of the earth, however, and modern theories from studying stars and planets, the earth was formed about 4.7 billion years ago, and is due to be exploded into gas when the sun explodes about 10 or 12 billion years from now, as a flaring nova; and so the statement is not true. But these are very long times in the existence of a species of life on the earth, and nearly every human being relies completely on the fallacy "The sun will rise tomorrow." The statement is, rather, a "hasty generalization," a "jumping to a conclusion."

8 FALLACIES OF NEGLECTED ASPECT

Hasty generalization / jumping to a conclusion

Composition / attempting to reason from each part to an organized whole

Division / attempting to reason from an organized whole to each part

Post Hoc / post hoc ergo propter hoc / attempting to reason from A followed by B that A is the cause of B

Special Pleading / in English legal practice a special pleader presents only one side of a case

Oversimplification / presenting an argument in terms too simple to cover all issues

Black-or-White Fallacy / false dilemma / ignoring intermediate positions

Argument of the Beard / using the middle ground to avoid admission of real differences (how many whiskers make a beard?)

7 FALLACIES OF GENERAL IRRELEVANCE

Diversion / a wandering from the subject

Extension / exaggeration of an opponent's position in such a way as to make it easier to attack

Misuse of Humor / replacing an argument by a wisecrack, choking off further thought

Argumentum ad Ignorantium / making use of the failure to prove one side of an argument as evidence to supposedly prove the opposite side

Argumentum ad Baculum / argument by appeal to the club / "your money or your life"

Argumentum ad Hominem / argument based on attacking the quality of the man who proposes something

Pettifogging / quibbling, concentrating on petty issues, diverting attention from important issues

6 FALLACIES OF COUNTERFEIT EVIDENCE

Meaning from Association / orchids, diamonds, or movie stars for selling alcohol

Repeated Assertion / "It is easier to believe a lie repeated 50 times than a fact one has never heard of before"

Prestige Jargon / "suffers from circumorbital haetoma" for "has a black eye"

Confident Manner / "every day in every way I am getting better and better"

Cliche Thinking / "nothing venture, nothing win" vs. "better be safe than sorry"

Rationalizing / giving good reasons instead of real reasons; justifying mistakes and errors by excusing one's self, "it could not have been avoided"

5 FALLACIES OF SUBJECTIVE IRRELEVANCE

These come from the tendency of human beings to be guided by feeling instead of reason.

Decision by Indecision / refusal to decide may determine what happens

Misuse of Emotional Words / Bertand Russell's "conjugation" of an "irregular verb": I am firm — You are obstinate — He is pig-headed"

Argumentum ad Misericordiam / appeal to sympathy and pity, appeal of the beggar

Attitude Fitting / the salesman who adjusts his salestalk to the moods and views of each prospect

Argumentum ad Populum / the politician who tells his listeners in emotional words what they want to hear

6 FALLACIES OF FALSE PRESUMPTION

Anything we take for granted may be called a presumption. A false presumption is something taken for granted that is not true.

Misuse of the Golden Mean / To take a position because it is moderate between two extremes irrespective of the nature of the positions is misuse of the ancient Greek principle of "the golden mean"

Contradictory Assumptions / "it took him a long time to read the illegible letter"

Misuse of Analogy / argument by analogy is primitive, common, fertile, useful, inevitable, and dangerous: because analogies are regularly incomplete

Begging the Question / "A good man is a man who is good" / "I set my wrist watch by my electric clock, and my electric clock by my wrist watch"

Poisoning the Wells / "You talk too much" "The more you talk, the more you prove you talk too much"

Hypothesis Contrary to Fact / "If the American Revolution had not happened..." etc. — no conclusions can be drawn

6 FALLACIES OF THE MISUSE OF LANGUAGE

Words are the symbols of objects and ideas; thoughts can be transferred efficiently and accurately only when words mean the same thing to speaker and hearer.

Equivocation / the use of a word in two different senses / "I have a mind to try it." Repartee: "Yes, nothing is wanting but the mind."

Obfuscation / a darkening or obscuring / usually accomplished by a maze of words

Leading Question / "Do you still beat your wife?"

Lifting Out of Context / using a quotation or statement without the original stipulated conditions

False Obversion / misuse of contrasts or opposites / "that is a woman driver for you"

False Conversion / interchanging subject and predicate / "all freshmen are students" vs. "all students are freshmen" / "no rats are people" vs. "no people are rats"

6 FALLACIOUS SYLLOGISMS OF THE SENATOR JOSEPH R. MCCARTHY (1908–1957) TYPE

All Communists defend Russia.
John Jones defends Russia.
Therefore John Jones is a Communist.

All caterpillars eat lettuce.
Sam Smith eats lettuce.
Therefore Sam Smith is a caterpillar.

All Communists favor three meals a day.
John Jones favors three meals a day.
Therefore John Jones is a Communist.

All successful men work hard.
Bill Brown works hard.
Therefore Bill Brown is successful.

All lazy workers get fired.
Charles Cowan got fired.
Therefore Charles Cowan is a lazy worker.

All monkeys climb trees.
My son climbs trees.
Therefore my son is a monkey.

12 Computers and Probability, Statistics, Guessing, Estimating...

THE MATHEMATICAL WORLD AND THE REAL WORLD

Who has not heard the remark "there are liars, damn liars, and statistics"? And, when one adds to this situation the power of a computer, with its capacity to perform more than 50 million operations in a minute, the evil brew may become misleading, dangerous, and poisonous.

Accordingly, this book needs to emphasize the basic elements of the successful use of probability and statistics, with computers and without computers.

A good way to do this is to emphasize the relationship between probability and statistics — the mathematical concepts — on the one hand, and the real world — physical reality, observations, experiments, evidence, and common sense — on the other.

THE IMPORTANCE OF PROBABILITY AND STATISTICS

All our lives we use many of the ideas of probability and statistics, often without clearly understanding more than a little about them. We say, "I think it is probably going to rain today," or "Bill is late for dinner more often than not," or "The odds are 7 to 5 that Harvard will beat Yale next week." Words and phrases like "probably, likely, often, seldom, almost always, almost never, the chance is good that ..., I'll bet a nickel that ...," and many others in our ordinary, everyday language show how often we consider probabilities and statistics.

These subjects are also the basis of the weighing of risks and the business of insurance. More than 2000 years ago, in the days of ancient Rome, merchants whose ships were sailing the seas would make contracts with bankers whereby the merchant would agree to pay a certain part of the profit from a voyage to the banker on condition that the banker pay him a certain amount of money to cover his loss should the voyage result in a shipwreck. This was the beginning of insurance. In France during the 1600's, gambling was popular in the court of the French king, and the mathematician Pascal was asked to compute the odds of winning or losing in certain games. At that time the theory of probability took its first exact mathematical form.

Nowadays the science of probability and statistics is of immense practical value. All of the insurance business is based on mathematical chances of certain events happening — death, damage, accident, and so on.

In every business, managers must weigh risks and estimate the chances of certain hazards when making important decisions. For example, an automobile manufacturer might make 200,000 cars expecting to sell them all; if he only sold 100,000 he might well go bankrupt from his mistake in estimating a chance. Businessmen who can correctly estimate future chances and trends have a substantial advantage in competition.

The government of the United States and many other organizations publish great quantities of statistics. These statistics deal with people, manufactured goods, the output of farms, the weather, business conditions, stock market prices, wholesale price changes, and a host of other subjects. These statistics are carefully studied by many thousands of interested persons, each of whom wants to estimate the probable future by knowing the certain past.

(Source: *Probability and Statistics: An Introduction Through Experiments* by Edmund C. Berkeley, published by Berkeley Enterprises Inc., 815 Washington Street, Newtonville, Mass. 02160, fifth printing, 1974, xvi + 121 pp)

45 COMMONLY OCCURRING NOUNS AND ADJECTIVES REFERRING TO PROBABILITY AND STATISTICS

abnormal
bet
certain
chance

common
estimate
estimated
eternal
evanescent
event
example
expected
expectation
experiment

failure
flip
frequency
frequent
guess
guessed

hazard
hazardous
impossible
improbable
irregular

likely
normal
observation
odds
outcome

possible
probable
random
rare
regular

risk
risky
sample
success
toss

uncommon
unlikely
unusual
usual
wager

25 VERBS REFERRING TO PROBABILITY AND STATISTICS

bet
can
cannot
estimate
expect

experiment
fail
flip

gamble
guess
happen
hazard
may
must
observe

occur
risk
roll
sample
succeed

test
throw
toss
try
wager

23 ADVERBS REFERRING TO PROBABILITY AND STATISTICS

abnormally
always
certainly
commonly
eternally

forever
frequently
intermittently
irregularly
maybe

never
normally
often
possibly
probably

rarely
regularly
seldom
sometimes
uncommonly

uncertainly
unusually
usually

A FREQUENCY DISTRIBUTION

Let us make an experiment, which we shall call Experiment No. 1. We take an unbiased coin, flip it six times, and count the number of heads that appear. We might, for example, obtain an outcome of two heads and four tails. We repeat the experiment, say, 100 times, and call this Series No. 1. Now we classify the experiments in Series No. 1 according to the number of heads that appear in each experiment, and we shall arrive at a table that will look very much like Table 1.

Table 1

Number of Heads	Number of Experiments
0	1
1	10
2	23
3	31
4	25
5	8
6	2
Total	100

This is a good example of a frequency distribution.

The next thing we need is names — letters are usually the most convenient — for naming the features of a frequency distribution. These names appear in Table 2.

Table 2

x, the observed or measured variable, the number of heads	f, the frequency, the number of experiments	F, the cumulative frequency
0	1	1
1	10	11
2	23	34
3	31	65
4	25	90
5	8	98
6	2	100
i, the total number of different values of x possible: 7	N, the total frequency: 100	

In general, a frequency distribution, when observed in experiments, consists of a number of values of x, an independent observed variable, together with, for each value of x, the number of observations of that value of x, its frequency, f. The different values of x are often equally spaced. The total number of the different values of x, usually called i, generally ranges from 2 to 20 or 25. If i is larger, it is often useful to condense or group the distribution so that i becomes smaller: we adopt fewer values of x, and add the corresponding frequencies. There is often not much loss of information from such grouping.

The total frequency, usually called N, may of course be any positive number, depending on how many experiments are included in the series. There is no loss of information, however, from making a note of the observed N, and changing the frequencies in the table proportionately so that the total is any convenient number. For our purposes, numerical information will regularly be reported as if N were 100, and algebraic information will regularly be reported as if N were 1. If N is 1, there is no difference between probability and theoretical statistical frequency; if N is not one, they are proportional.

The sign Σ (capital Greek S, called "sigma") means "sum". For example, the total frequency, $N = \Sigma f$. The cumulative frequency, often called F, is the sum of the frequency up to and including any value of x. F is in many cases useful, because often when f is not simple, F may be, and vice versa.

(Source: *A Summary of Probability Distributions* by Edmund C. Berkeley, revised edition, third printing, published by Berkeley Enterprises Inc., 815 Washington Street, Newtonville, Mass. 02160, 1959)

18 TECHNICAL TERMS ABOUT A DISTRIBUTION OF CASES IN STATISTICS

experiment

unbiased

coin

flip

heads

tails

series of experiments

classification

x, the observed or measured variable, the number of heads

f, the frequency, the number of experiments showing x

F, the cumulative frequency

i, the total number of different values of x possible, the number of classes resulting from the classification

N, the total frequency, the sum of the f's

1, certainty, the sum of the f's divided by N

f/N, theoretical relative statistical frequency, or the probability of observing the occurrence of x

m, the mean, equal to x times f summed divided by N

variance, the sum of the squares of the deviations from the mean each weighted by the frequency, all divided by N

σ, the standard deviation, the square root of the variance

PATTERNS OF DISTRIBUTIONS OF PROBABILITY — AND MODELS FOR UNDERSTANDING PATTERNS OF EVENTS

Books, of course, have been written on the definitions of probability. The definition that we shall use is "theoretical relative statistical frequency". In other words, the probability of some "favorable" happening is the limit approached in theory by the ratio of the number of "favorable" happenings to the total number of both "favorable" and "unfavorable" happenings. For example, suppose we repeatedly toss a coin that appears to be evenly balanced and flat on both sides. We theorize that if we make more and more tosses, the ratio of the total number of heads to the total number of both heads and tails will come ever closer to ½. So ½ is the probability of heads, the "theoretical relative statistical frequency" of heads.

Depending on the types of series of events that we may study in the real world, we obtain different patterns of theoretical statistical frequencies, different probability distributions. Most textbooks on statistics discuss two of these probability distributions — the two known as the "normal" and the "binomial" — but they say little about many others. It is, however, useful to know about other probability distributions, because then we have in our minds a broader collection of models for understanding the patterns of events in the real world.

A word about the level of knowledge assumed. A fair amount of the information here can be understood by persons who know algebra, analytic geometry, and some statistics. For a complete understanding of the information here, however, a knowledge of calculus is also needed.

(Source: *A Summary of Probability Distributions* by Edmund C. Berkeley revised edition, third printing, published by Berkeley Enterprises Inc., 815 Washington St., Newtonville, Mass. 02160, 1959; all later information in this chapter, if not specified otherwise, is from this source)

11 PATTERNS OF DISTRIBUTION OF EVENTS, AND ILLUSTRATIONS

Distribution	Illustration
Binomial Distribution	Flipping coins
Normal Distribution	Measuring distances
Poisson Distribution	Scattering seed in plots
Uniform Distribution	Classifying digits
Cauchy Distribution	Spraying particles from a center
Pascal's Distribution	Rolling dice until 7 or 11
Polya's Distribution	Motorists losing licenses
Causal Distribution	Dissolving a little sugar in a lot of water

Chi-Squared Distribution	Judging departures from randomness
Student's Distribution	Estimating population means from sample means
Life Table Distribution	Estimating the survival of people, telephone poles, radioactive elements, ...

8 PRINCIPLES FOR GUESSING AND ESTIMATING

To find the sum of N numbers, guess at a middle number, and multiply by N.

To find the product of N numbers, separate each number into a digit and a power of 10. Then multiply the digits and total the zeros in the powers of 10

To extract the square root of N, find the square next below and the square next above. Then choose an in-between square root. Test it. Then improve your guess.

To cross a street with traffic in both directions, estimate your path and the paths of the vehicles, and then decide. If the traffic is too dense, wait for a green light for crossing.

By cultivating your sense of time, you can guess rather closely how much time has gone by since the last time you saw a clock. And you can always spot a wrong clock.

By noticing the direction of the sun, the time of day and the expected travel of the sun and shadows, you can cultivate your sense of directions.

When lost in hills and woods, follow downgrades and stream beds to probable roads and probable houses.

Cultivate a tentative viewpoint about all new calculations and new propositions, and seek to test them by common sense, elementary and advanced. Advanced common sense includes science and wisdom.

13 Computers and Education, Philosophy, and the World

COMPUTERS AND AN EDUCATED PERSON

On one occasion some twenty years ago I tried to explain what I thought was an educated person. The definition I offered was that an educated person:

1. is able to read and write, and do arithmetic;
2. has a basic knowledge of the history and geography of the world and of humankind;
3. understands the scientific method, and has an elementary knowledge of physics, chemistry, biology, and anthropology;
4. has an elementary knowledge of mathematics and logic, what they are, and how to use them;
5. knows at least one other language besides his or her own well enough to read and talk a little in it;
6. can say what he or she means in suitable words, both speaking and writing;
7. is able to do work that is socially useful;
8. is able to listen, knows how to learn, and enjoys learning;
9. is curious and eager to find out answers to significant questions;
10. can find out alternatives and choose reasonably among them;
11. never forgets that his or her views and opinions may be wrong;
12. is always ready to change his or her views and opinions on good evidence.

Each one of these specifications has this property: I cannot classify or consider that a person is educated if he or she is lacking that property. For example, take specification 8: if she or he does not enjoy learning, I cannot consider that he or she is educated. Or take specification 11: if the person insists that all her or his significant views and opinions are "evidently" correct, then I cannot consider that that person is educated.

Clearly, this definition changes over time. For example, 300 years ago, in 1683, specifications 3 and 4 would not apply. In 1983, it is appropriate to assert that a person may be classified as educated only if that person:

1. has some knowledge of computers and
2. considers that he or she can know and understand computers to some extent.

I believe that any person Y who insists that Y cannot know or understand a subject X is uneducated. The position that one cannot acquire knowledge and understanding about any subject X reveals a lack of education. At least some knowledge and some understanding can be acquired about any subject X, including computers.

In regard to the first assertion, a number of colleges, universities, and other schools have taken a new position. They have added the following to the definition of an educated person:

13. has an elementary knowledge of computers and some experience with them.

I believe the first college where this position was taken was Dartmouth College during the 1960's, undoubtedly as a result of the influence of President John Kemeny and Dr. Thomas E. Kurtz. It would be interesting to know how many universities, colleges, and schools have adopted the principle that any graduate from their school has to have an elementary knowledge of computers and some experience with them.

(Source: editorial by Edmund C. Berkeley in *Computers and People,* May-June, 1983)

12 TOPICS WHICH COMPUTER SCIENCE COLLEGE PROFESSORS (PhD's) ARE REGULARLY NOT TAUGHT, AND WHICH EDUCATION MAJORS (EdD's) ARE REGULARLY TAUGHT

Topics / Determine the important topics that need to be covered in the course.

Ideas / Distinguish the main ideas and the less important ideas, and classify them.

Time / Adjust the amount of time spent teaching to the importance of ideas.

Objectives / Determine the precise outcomes or capacities that the student should desirably achieve from taking the course.

Classification / Assemble the objectives in systematic groups and classes.

Measurement / Develop tests or measures of the progress of each student and apply them at scheduled times — weekly, monthly, and final.

Student Vocabulary / Determine the level of the students' vocabularies and adjust the level of presentation to the student audience.

Response and Feedback / Watch the nonverbal communication of responses: attention or restlessness; eagerness or vacant faces; how many students are dozing; etc.

Integrating / Make clear and definite the relation of the presentation to other areas of the student's interests and studies. The student must take on the burden of determining the problems in his own field, of increasing complexity, to be solved by the instruction he is receiving. He is to identify them; he is not to be spoon-fed.

Participation Progress / The student needs to go beyond listening, note-taking, memorizing, reciting (regurgitating). He needs to find applications in his special areas and relate what he learns to those areas, and think about them.

Alternative Solutions / The student needs to examine and explore alternative solutions, not plump for the first solution that he thinks of.

Brainstorming / The student needs to ask "What if?" and compare and think about many different solutions (including "impossible" solutions).

7 OBJECTIVES FOR COMPUTER LITERACY REGARDING HARDWARE

Identify the five major components of a computer: input equipment; memory unit; control unit; arithmetic unit; output equipment

Identify the basic operation of a computer system: input of data or information; processing of data or information; output of data or information

Distinguish between hardware and software

Identify how a person can access a computer, such as via a keyboard terminal at the site of a computer or via a telephone line at any distance, or via punched or marked cards, or via magnetic media such as tape or diskette

Recognize the rapid growth of computer hardware since the 1940's

Determine that the basic components function as an interconnected system under the control of a stored program developed by a person

Compare computer processing and storage to the human brain, listing some general likenesses and differences

(Source: Minnesota Educational Computing Consortium, 2520 Broadway Drive, St. Paul, MN 55113)

7 OBJECTIVES FOR COMPUTER LITERACY REGARDING PROGRAMMING AND ALGORITHMS

Recognize the definition of "algorithm"

Follow and give the correct output for a simple algorithm

Given a simple algorithm explain what it accomplishes (that is, interpret and generalize)

Modify a simple algorithm to accomplish a new but related task

Detect logic errors in an improperly functioning algorithm

Develop an algorithm for solving a specific problem

Develop an algorithm which can be used to solve a set of similar problems

Note: The student should be able to accomplish these objectives when the algorithm is expressed as a set of English language instructions and in the form of a computer program.

(Source: same as previous)

Recognize that computers process data by searching, sorting, updating, summarizing, moving, etc.

Select an appropriate attribute for ordering of data for a particular task

Design an elementary data structure for a given application (that is, provide order for the data)

Design an elementary coding system for a given application

(Source: same as previous)

13 COMPUTER LITERACY OBJECTIVES REGARDING SOFTWARE AND DATA PROCESSING

Identify the fact that we communicate with computers through a binary code

Identify the need that data be organized if it is to be useful

Identify the fact that information is data that has been given meaning

Identify the fact that data is a coded mechanism for communication

Identify the fact that communication is the transmission of information via coded messages

Identify the fact that data processing involves the transformation of data by means of a set of predefined rules

Recognize that a computer needs instructions to operate

Recognize that a computer gets instructions from a program written in a programming language

Recognize that a computer is able to store a program and data

10 COMPUTER LITERACY OBJECTIVES REGARDING APPLICATIONS

Recognize specific uses of computers in some of the following fields: medicine / law enforcement / education / engineering / business / transportation / military defense systems / weather prediction / recreation / government / the library / creative arts

Identify the fact that there are many programming languages suitable for a particular application for business or science

Recognize that the following activities are among the major types of applications of the computer: information storage and retrieval / simulation and modeling / process control / decision-making / computation / data processing

Recognize that computers are generally good at information processing tasks that benefit from: speed / accuracy / repetitiveness

Recognize that some limiting considerations for using computers are: cost / software availability / storage capacity

Recognize the basic features of a computerized information system

Determine how computers can assist the consumer

Determine how computers can assist in a decision-making process

Assess the feasibility of potential applications

Develop a new application

(Source: same as previous)

16 COMPUTER LITERACY OBJECTIVES REGARDING THE SOCIAL IMPACT OF COMPUTERS

Distinguish among the following careers: keypuncher (or key operator) / computer operator / computer programmer / systems analyst / computer scientist

Recognize that computers are used to commit a wide variety of serious crimes; especially stealing money, stealing information

Recognize that identification codes (numbers) and passwords are a primary means for restricting use of: computer systems / computer programs / data files

Recognize that procedures for detecting computer-based crimes are not well developed

Identify some advantages or disadvantages of a data base containing personal information on a large number of people (for example, research value, potential privacy invasion)

Recognize several regulatory rules (for example, right to review one's own files, no universal personal identifiers)

Recognize that most privacy problems exist whether or not files are computerized

Recognize that computerization decreases some employment, increases other employment

Recognize that computerization personalizes some education (and other fields) and depersonalizes other education (etc.)

Recognize that computerization can lead to both greater independence of and greater dependence on one's tools

Recognize that computers can modify their own instruction set, display much "artificial intelligence", and learn

Recognize that many alleged "computer mistakes" are mistakes made by people

Plan a strategy for tracing and correcting a computer-related error (example, in billing)

Explain how computers make surveillance of the public more feasible

Recognize that every person is being affected indirectly in many sectors of social behavior by computerization

Explain how computers can be used to affect the distribution and use of economic and political power

(Source: same as previous)

9 COMPUTER LITERACY OBJECTIVES REGARDING ATTITUDES, VALUES, MOTIVATION

Does not feel fear, anxiety, or intimidation from computer experiences

Feels confident about his or her ability to use and control computers

Values efficient information processing, provided that it does not neglect accuracy, the protection of individual rights, and social needs

Values computerization of routine tasks, so long as it frees people to engage in other activities, and is not done as an end in itself

Values more communication and more availability of information possible through computers, provided it does not violate personal rights to privacy or the accuracy of personal data

Values economic benefits of computerization for a society

Likes and wants work or play with computers, especially computer-assisted learning

Describes past experiences with computers with positive-affect words like fun, exciting, challenging, etc.

Spends some free time using a computer, if given an opportunity

(Source: same as previous)

COMPUTERS AND THE FOUNTAIN OF YOUTH

Ponce de Leon, a Spanish explorer who discovered Florida lived from about 1460 until 1521. He is rather famous for hunting in America for the "Fountain of Youth". The water of this fountain or spring, it was reputed, would prolong the youth of the persons who drank from it. This fantasy led Ponce de Leon to spend many years of his life searching for it.

Now, in general, it seems to me there are two ways to prolong youth.

One way is to discover or invent a chemical — we might call it the youth hormone — that actually lengthens the period of youth, the number of years that extend from birth to sexual maturity (this is a convenient measure of youth applicable throughout the animal kingdom). Nature has discovered this chemical. The ordinary period of youth for a great many species of animals is only a year or two. A dog or a cat can become mature in this period; a rabbit, much sooner still. But for man, Nature has made use of the youth hormone to lengthen the ordinary duration of youth to about 14 or 15 years. The evolutionary advantage for a creature that needs to learn language and culture in order to survive is clearly evident.

The other way to prolong youth is to put many more experiences into the same amount of time. For example, one of the possible great advantages of television and videotapes, if they are wisely used, could be to give five times as much instruction to a young person in an hour as would otherwise happen.

An interactive computer program implies individual personal instruction, and individualized useful experiences in great quantity. Instruction from an interactive computer can often be far better than the usual instruction from a teacher.

Another advantage from the interactive computer is to make possible experiments and trials that cannot otherwise be performed in the real world. There is a remarkable passage in a book called *An Executive's Guide to Computer Concepts* by Powell and Monsma. The authors describe an occasion when an engineer for the first time enjoyed the fruit of a new computer program for the engineering design of a type of turbine. This engineer sat at the computer console for about 20 minutes, and experimented with the design of various types of turbines. Then he rose from the console, turned to one of the authors of the book, and said, "I have learned more about the design of this kind of turbine in the last twenty minutes than I have previously learned in the last twenty years."

With only tables in a handbook to rely on, he had had to choose very conservative designs. But the easy simulation of the operation of turbines, without the large cost of real models and physical testing, the possible hazards and dangers of failure when running — had given him the answers to questions that he had never been able to investigate.

It seems to me that computers, applied to benefiting youth and increasing knowledge, will eventually enable young people to achieve double or quadruple the amount of learning and the amount of experience which they would otherwise be able to achieve — a veritable fountain of youth, though hardly what Ponce de Leon imagined.

(Source: from an editorial by Edmund C. Berkeley in *Computers and People* for April, 1978)

BOOKS, COMPUTERS, AND THE GREAT FUTURE

One way of thinking about a computer is to think of it as a kind of book.

Output. A book (for example, in Russian) contains information which you can read, provided you know the spoken language (Russian) and the alphabet (of Russian), and can pronounce the alphabetic signs (in context) that spell the designated words. In the same way a computer contains information which can be output usefully, provided you know the set of operations by means of which the computer will produce the information you desire.

Input. You can put information into a book. For a simple example, you can make entries in your date book, or put notes into a notebook, or even write a manuscript which a publisher will print as a book. In the same way, you can put information into a computer — give it data and programming by means of which later you can get useful information out.

Storage. You can store information in a book. In fact, a book is a magnificent way of storing information. The sheets of paper it comprises can be easily impressed with marks that will stay a few days or a few centuries. The sheets of paper with their marks can be easily duplicated in quantity and spread all over the world. You can store information in a computer, not as well all in all, but effectively. Of course, most of the time the storage cannot be sensed by human beings; only by magnetic changes and electronic pulses can human beings find out the information stored in the computer. But the techniques are becoming so widespread that one nowadays hears few complaints that "you cannot see what is in the computer."

Calculation.   You can calculate with a book. Books are full of tables of results — for many varieties and combinations of many kinds of data. In this way, they effectively provide many calculations that exactly fit the requirements. A great many more calculations than those stored in books can be done by a man with a book of factors in his pocket and some rules for estimating stored in his brain. In this way the man may be ready to inspect, and approve or disapprove, all kinds of calculated results.

However, a computer really comes into its own when it is a matter of calculating and deciding about more elaborate cases than can ever be tabulated in books or decided by educated inspection.

Ideas.   But when we think of ideas, of knowledge, we think of books.

The knowledge written down and printed in books is still the foundation of all present-day civilization. This is true for many reasons. First, quantity: The amount of useful information recorded in print is enormously greater than the amount of useful information expressed in all the other ways put together. Any story, epic, adventure, idea, principle, science, philosophy, art, technique, discovery, technology, once written down and printed, can be read, studied, and learned from books. Second, accessibility: It is quite easy and cheap to get or borrow a copy of almost any book on almost any subject whenever you want to read it — far easier and cheaper than to obtain access to a computer and communicate with it. Third, convenience: You can take what the book says into your own mind at your own time at your own speed. If you want to hurry and skip, you can; if you want to read it over and over until you know it by heart, you can; if you want to read it on a commuting train in the morning, you can. In a book you can communicate with another mind, not at its speed or convenience, but at your own. Fourth, quality: In books, the greatest men who have ever lived, the best experts, the most informed authorities, can offer you answers for your questions, instruction in the subjects you are most concerned with, guidance in the problems that rack your spirit, and far more. Fifth, vicarious experience: You and I will probably never climb Mt. Everest, or survive the sinking of an ocean liner, or look through a porthole at a kind of starfish seven miles down in the Pacific Ocean. We shall certainly never flee from Pompeii while Vesuvius erupts, or accompany Charles Darwin on the survey ship Beagle around South America. Yet reading a book at our leisure, we can become oblivious to the real world around us and feel and imagine ourselves having such experiences. The treasury of the wisdom and knowledge of the world is in books. And the gateway is open to anyone who can read.

The computer field is still enormously involved with machinery, circuits, equipment, optical character reading, interfaces, modems, maintenance, etc.,

etc., etc. But we can predict that as the years pass, all this will fade into the background, and the foreground of attention will be the content and ideas of computer programs and data bases, the knowledge they contain, and the power to answer questions which they express.

Which is more important, the manufacture of books or the content of books? — the manufacture of computers or the content of computers? The answers are obvious.

So we can confidently predict that in the future the computer field will be something like an automatic social mind containing concepts, ideas, programs, systems, and other intellectual constructs by means of which almost all knowledge, and records of experiences of almost all kinds, can be studied, investigated, manipulated, summarized, and communicated to individual human minds. The treasury of the knowledge of the world will become automated.

Here is where the future lies.

This view, outward bound, is very exciting. This development may even contain the solutions to many giant problems which human beings of today, with their own little abilities, and their even more limited memories, and their slowly accessible, passive, storehouses of books called libraries, cannot be expected to solve.

(Source: from an editorial by Edmund C. Berkeley in *Computers and Automation* for January, 1971)

EXAMPLES, UNDERSTANDING, AND COMPUTERS

How does a human being take in an idea and use it?

How does a human being take in ideas about computers and computer programming, and thereby understand computers and computer programs?

How do we arrange this process of understanding so that it becomes much more efficient than it used to be, and so that we overcome one of the greatest bottlenecks in the use of computers — understanding them and their programs?

Some months ago, I watched a squirrel raid a bird feeder. The bird feeder was an inverted glass cylinder, with a wide, sloping, conical lid to keep out rain, and a round base trough, into which sunflower seeds and other seeds fed slowly by gravity through openings. The feeder was tied by a short string to a pole; the pole rested in a forsythia bush projecting about two feet beyond the bush. When I first saw the squirrel, he was investigating and eating some of the fallen sunflower seeds on the ground below the bird feeder, and then he rose up and tried to reach the bird feeder from the ground; but it was too high for him, and he could not reach it. A little bit later, I saw him crawling out on the pole towards the bird feeder. Then, holding on to the pole with his right hind paw only, he lowered himself slowly along the bird feeder, preventing it from swinging out with his left hind paw. He stretched his full length upside down towards the base of the feeder, got his front paws on the seeds, and proceeded to eat all he wanted for about five minutes, remaining head downward. Finally, he drew himself back up to the pole, and left along the pole through the bush.

I would say that the squirrel had a good idea, and I would say that the squirrel understood the situation!

The squirrel's idea, however, is not demonstrable, because I cannot look into the squirrel's mind, and of course he cannot tell me anything about what is in his mind. We do not speak each other's language. But the squirrel's understanding is demonstrable: he showed he was able to perceive relevant features of the situation, adapt means to ends, and fulfill his goal.

Often, when I have access to a computer, I am like that squirrel. I run a program, present data, and try to get what I want out of the computer, but at first nothing desirable happens. The goal is out of reach, over my head. On later trials with a different procedure, I may have more success. I remember one case last spring: to make sure that I could use a certain assembly program correctly, I very carefully copied out on punched paper tape a simple symbolic example given in the published manual. But it would not assemble, even on repeated efforts. Finally, somebody nearby remarked that maybe there should be a carriage return character at the end of the symbolic tape — though there was nothing whatever said about that in the manual. With that change, the symbolic example in the manual assembled immediately. My understanding remained incomplete until my sample case actually operated correctly.

To the extent that I can give the computer data regarding a situation or problem that I am interested in, and get back from the computer certain results that I want — to that extent I understand the computer. My understanding increases in terms of the quantity and variety of instances, examples, cases, problems, situations, that I can operate with. The more different kinds of sample problems I can solve on the computer, the more I understand it.

It seems to be true that animals in general take in ideas and increase their understanding, from examples, experiences. Chickens learn from examples that they are fed corn at the end of the day in the chicken yard, and they come running back from foraging to get it. Professor B. F. Skinner of Harvard trains a pigeon to peck in the pattern of a figure 8 by giving it little rewards for each increase in sample behavior toward the desired pattern.

Men have an advantage over animals in that ideas may be conveyed by language as well as examples. But over and over again men build up their understanding of ideas by means of examples, illustrations, and models, rather than language. We gain a firsthand understanding of probability by experimenting with flipping coins and rolling dice. We increase our understanding of how to drive a car by dealing with many examples of driving situations in the real world, ranging from simple ones in driver training courses to more complicated ones in independent driving in difficult traffic. Certainly one of the best ways to produce full understanding of computers and computer programming would be well-designed sequences of examples from simple to complex, together with access to a computer to try them on!

(Source: from an editorial by Edmund C. Berkeley in *Computers and Automation* for December, 1964)

7 FRONTIERS OF RESEARCH AND DEVELOPMENT FOR COMPUTERS AND THEIR APPLICATION

Reading machine / to teach illiterate and semi-literate persons to read, read well, and enjoy reading / reading teacher

Training machine / to instruct persons who do not know how to do some task just how to do it / job trainer

Idea processor / to process all the ideas in the language and discussion pertaining to a subject, as mathematicians process numbers / thinker, philosopher, expert, consultant

Recognizing machine / to look at or sense entities in their environments and determine what they signify / driver of a car, bus, or truck

Generalizing machine / to look at or sense a number of instances and see what meanings are to be deducted from those instances / researcher, scientist, cryptanalyst

Robot / to act with all the flexibility of the generalized animal body and to sense with all the variety of animal senses / generalized manipulator

Anti-danger machine / to sense heat, cold, opening, closing, motion, time of day, etc.; to deduce conditions of danger, intrusion, etc.; to report quickly / policeman, owner, guard

18 PROPERTIES OF THE WORD AND CONCEPT "PROCESS"

Definitions:

a progress or advance; a forward or onward movement; a progress in development

something going on; a proceeding

a procedure; a particular way of accomplishing something or of acting; a series of steps followed in a regular definite order

a natural phenomenon marked by gradual changes that lead toward a particular result

a series of actions or operations conducing to an end

a continuous operation or treatment, especially in manufacture

Similes:

A process is often like a chain.

A process is often like a black box.

A process is often like a network.

A process is often like a journey.

A process is sometimes like a military campaign.

A process is sometimes like an explosion.

Examples:

The growth of a child is a process.

The construction of a building is a process.

The evolution of living species is a process.

The assembly of an automobile is a process.

The education of a man is a process.

A method of computing is a process.

10 PRONOUNCEMENTS BY THE PHILOSOPHER BERTRAND RUSSELL

Philosophy from the earliest times, has made greater claims, and achieved fewer results that any other branch of learning.

Our age is one of bewildered groping where our ancestors walked in the clear daylight of unquestioning certainty.

The Greek philosophers believed in the omnipotence of reasoning.

The discovery of geometry intoxicated them, and its deductive method appeared capable of universal application.

They proved:
all reality is one;
there is no such thing as change;
the world of sense is a world of mere illusion.

The strangeness of their results gave them no qualms because they believed in the correctness of their reasoning.

As the vital impulse of the early philosophers died away, its place was taken by authority and tradition, reinforced in the Middle Ages and later by systematic theology.

The true function of logic is to liberate the imagination as to what the world may be — but not to legislate as to what the world is.

To the medieval schoolmen, who lived amid wars, massacres, and pestilences, nothing appeared so delightful as safety and order.

Evolutionism, in one form or another, is the prevailing creed of our time.

(Source: *Our Knowledge of the External World*, pp 3 to 11, by Bertrand Russell publ. by W.W. Norton & Co., New York, 1929, 268 pp)

5 STAGGERING CHANGES IN THE WORLD OF HUMANITY DURING THE 1900's

Nuclear Energy: before 1945 man could not obtain energy from the nucleus of atoms / after 1945 man could

Space Travel: before 1957 man could not voyage to the moon and the planets / after 1957 he could

Computers: before 1944 man could not delegate long intricate flexible sequences of reasonable operations on information to machines / after 1944 man could

National Sovereignty: before 1981 man could tolerate unlimited sovereignty of nation-states to make unlimited war / after 1981 man decided this is no longer tolerable

Nuclear Holocaust: before 1955 man could not destroy the earth and all life in it / after 1955 he could

THE NINE MOST IMPORTANT PROBLEMS IN THE WORLD AND THEIR RELATION TO COMPUTERS

Somebody asked me what I thought were the most important problems in the world, and how computers could do something useful and constructive about them. My questioner and I agreed upon a definition: a most important problem in the world is a problem which, if not solved, will result in one of the following things:

1. millions of human beings will die; or
2. the environment which human beings need for living will disappear; or
3. the thinking and technology with which human beings can hope to solve the great problems of human survival cannot be attained.

An example is the problem of modern technology for weapons, which includes nuclear weapons as just one example of hideousness and disaster.

The stockpile of weapons in the possession of the United States is sufficient to destroy all human life on earth. The same is true of the stockpile of nuclear weapons in the possession of the Soviet Union. France, England, and China have demonstrated nuclear weapons. The "club" of nations that have nuclear weapons will expand further. Suppose another psychotic dictator like Hitler came to power in any country with nuclear weapons. Then before accepting defeat in a war he would use them. It is my belief that West Germany, India, Egypt, and Israel all now have nuclear weapons.

This condition constitutes a huge and fearful danger. "National security" by way of nuclear weapons has become a zero. Other avenues are needed.

Thirty three years after the time when one nuclear bomb was dropped by the United States in Hiroshima, Japan, in 1945, a realistic international solution seems hardly to have begun. Only an unnegotiated balance of terror exists, which can effectively restrain rational governments only.

Besides nuclear devices, many other very dangerous branches of modern weapons technology exist: chemical warfare, bacteriological warfare, radiological warfare, electronic warfare, psychological warfare, the covert warfare of intelligence agencies, etc. Recently a newspaper reported that Orwell's *1984* had been studied and about 100 of some 130 methods of warfare and oppression there forecast had now materialized. I feel rather glad that my death will probably come before the holocausts of the future.

No inventory of the most important problems of the world can be definitive — but I count nine of them, and here is my list:

1. Modern Technology for Weapons: as mentioned above.
2. War-Making Industry: the vested interest in war in almost every country in the world; the munition makers, owners, managers, workers, scientists, stockholders ... whose jobs and whose profits are linked to war.
3. The Population Explosion: leading to starvation and famine.
4. The Exhaustion of Resources — and its Result, Poverty: a condition in which the accumulated deposits (oil, iron, copper, etc.) of more than four

billion years are being exhausted in a century or two by so-called "modern" exploitation of the earth's resources.

5. Pollution of the Environment: as for example the continuing increase of carbon dioxide, lead, and other foreign materials in the atmosphere of the earth.

6. Waste: waste of food by eating too much, waste of paper and packaging by one-time use, waste of time and minds by television, etc.

7. Inadequacies of Language, Education, and Communications: so that great numbers of human beings cannot exchange ideas with each other, cannot discuss and resolve their differences, cannot easily appreciate the humanity of other human beings.

8. Advertising, Propaganda and Lies: the "information power" by which many vested interests exert control over the information allowed to reach the public.

9. Arresting the Tendency of People to Love Each Other — and What it Leads to: distrust, hatred, and genocide, such as 11 million Europeans killed by the Nazis, 1941–45; 2 million Armenians killed by the Turks, 1914–18; 650,000 Carthaginians killed by the Romans, 146 BC; ...

Of course, computers can apply to these problems, even as pencil and paper can; besides, they make possible investigation, appraisals, and decisions that are not possible with only pencil and paper.

A miraculous power that lies in microcomputers is automatic immediate translation from one language to another, so that the curse of the Tower of Babel will vanish. Already a vocabulary of 5000 words and phrases can be stored in an English-French microcomputer and translator. Later on there will be voice.

Much, much more can be explored and aided by computer.

The first steps in dealing with these nine great problems are:

to strip off their usual disguises;

to push them continually into the news, reducing, if necessary, coverage of sports, movie stars, cigarette advertising, etc.;

to help people everywhere to think about them, discuss them, agitate about them; and

to try to do something sensible about them.

"The evil that lies concealed is always the most serious."

-Publilius Syrus, 43 BC

(Source: editorial by Edmund C. Berkeley in *Computers and People* for March-April, 1979)

SILLY SCIENCE AND EVIL SCIENCE

Science, like history or art or technology or culture or education or law, is one of many long-term human interests and human activities, and produces an establishment. That establishment consists of persons who pursue science in many places, laboratories, universities, departments of businesses and governments, conferences, etc., all over the world. In the United States two of the main elements of the science establishment are the National Science Foundation and the American Association for the Advancement of Science. The leading officers of these organizations are "prestigious" in the current jargon of the media.

Now the regular and natural arrangement in any establishment is "you scratch my back and I'll scratch yours." From this comfortable and cooperative arrangement, it often follows (to borrow some of George Orwell's language in *Animal Farm*) "everybody's project is equal, but some projects are more equal than others." It is bad form, not cricket, to criticize the subject matter of any scientist's investigations. If he wants to work on a new programming language like ADA, fine. If he wants to study ants, fine. If he wants to discover the most cost-effective way to kill human beings with a nuclear bomb, fine — only call his occupation "defense" instead of "war" and the corpses "enemies" or "gooks" or "commies." In Nazi Germany, qualified medical doctors wrote scientific papers on how much broken glass could be inserted into the legs of Polish women without their dying. If the scientist wants to prove the four-color map problem by computer, call the subject "basic mathematical research"; and finally when it is proved by computer, an article is published in the "prestigious" scientific magazines.

The scientific establishment is not fulfilling all the needs of society.

What should we do?

It seems to me that there are four basic principles that we should recognize and put into the operations of science:

1. Not Hurt People: Science should not hurt people. Scientists should not devote their talents to war, or torture, or brainwashing, or harming people in any way. I hold as dishonorable those scientists who engage in these activities.
2. Not Hurt the Environment. Science should not hurt the environment. Of course, if mosquitoes are going to bite me and transfer to me the malaria plasmodium, I would eagerly wipe out that kind of mosquito and that kind of plasmodium. But there are hundreds of less severe and even good ways of dealing with insects and the environment, as I used to observe a long time ago when I would hike on the trails of the Appalachian Mountain Club in New Hampshire.

3. The Decrease of Poverty: I know there are at least a billion people in the world who do not have enough to eat, enough shelter, enough clothing. A portion of the time and energy of every scientist should be devoted to this problem. I hold as honorable those scientists, wherever they may be, who try scientifically to help people have more food, more shelter, more clothing, a better life.

4. The Navigation of the Fragile Spaceship Earth: All of us (mankind), and the biosphere without which we cannot survive, are together passengers on the earth going around the sun, one orbital revolution in each year, for (we hope) many thousands and millions of years to come. We must all live together, arrive at a *modus vivendi,* a way of living together. We have no other choice. The nuclear holocaust awaits. We must cooperatively solve our problems. If we don't like reds, or blacks, or yellows, or greens, or blues, we must still cooperatively solve our problems. Science should teach all of us how to do this, and never forget that this is now the chief mission of scientists.

The English scientist Thomas Henry Huxley said in 1870:

Life is a game which has been played for untold ages, every man and woman of us being one of the two players. The chessboard is the world; the pieces are the phenomena of the universe; the rules of the game are what we call the laws of Nature. The player on the other side is hidden from us. We know that he is fair, just, and patient. But also we know to our cost that he never overlooks a mistake, or makes the smallest allowance for ignorance.

(Source: from an editorial by Edmund C. Berkeley in *Computers and People* for Sept.-Oct., 1982)

AN ENGINEER'S HIPPOCRATIC OATH BY CHARLES SUSSKIND

I solemnly pledge myself to consecrate my life to the service of humanity. I will give to my teachers the respect and gratitude which is their due; I will be loyal to the profession of engineering and just and generous to its members; I will lead my life and practice my profession in uprightness and honor; whatever project I shall undertake, it shall be for the good of mankind to the utmost of my power; I will keep far aloof from wrong, from corruption, and from tempting others to vicious practice; I will exercise my profession solely for the benefit of humanity and perform no act for a criminal purpose, even if solicited, far less suggest it; I will speak out against evil and unjust practice wheresoever I encounter it; I will not permit considerations of religion, nationality, race, party politics, or social standing to intervene between my duty and my work; even under threat, I will not use my professional knowledge contrary to the laws of humanity; I will endeavor to avoid waste and consumption of nonrenewable resources. I make these promises solemly, freely, and upon my honor.

(Source: from *Understanding Technology* by Charles Susskind, published 1973 by The John Hopkins University Press, Baltimore, MD 21218)

Bibliography

Part 1

Bailey, Richard, *Computer Poems,* Potagannissing Press, Drummond Island, MI, 1973, 64 pp.

Davis, Philip J., *The Lore of Large Numbers,* publ. by Mathematical Association of America, 1529 18th St. NW, Washington, DC 20036, 12th printing, 1961, 165 pp.

Galler, Bernard A., and Alan J. Perlis, *A View of Programming Languages,* Addison-Wesley Publishing Co., Reading, MA 01867, 1970, 282 pp.

Gotlieb, C.C., and A. Borodin, *Social Issues in Computing,* Academic Press, 111 Fifth Avenue, New York, NY 10003, 1973, 284 pp.

Kucera, H., and W.N. Francis, *Computational Analysis of Present-Day American English,* Brown University Press, Providence, RI 02906, 1970, 424 pp.

Lehmer, Derrick Norman, *List of Prime Numbers,* Hafner Publishing Co., New York, NY, 2nd printing, 1956, 133 pp.

Lorenz, Konrad Z., *King Solomon's Ring: New Light on Animal Ways,* Thomas Y. Crowell Co., New York, NY, 1952, 202 pp.

Martin, Thomas L., Jr., *Malice in Blunderland,* McGraw-Hill Book Co., New York, NY, 1973, 143 pp.

McCollum, Douglas W., "A New Coding Format for Hard Copy Numeric Input," in *Computers and People,* July-August 1982, publ. by Berkeley Enterprises, Inc., Newtonville, MA 02160.

McGrath, R.R., Jr. and R.M. Stair, Jr., *Essentials of COBOL Programming,* Richard D. Irwin, Inc., Homewood, IL 60430, 1981, 82 pp.

Ogden, C.K., *The Basic Dictionary,* Kegan, Paul, Trench, Trubner, & Co., London, England, 1939, 106 pp.

Polya, G., *How to Solve It: A New Aspect of Mathematical Method,* Princeton University Press, Princeton, NJ 08540, 1945; 2nd edition, publ. by Doubleday & Co., Garden City, NY, 1957, 253 pp.

Ralston, Anthony, editor, and over 200 contributors, *Encyclopedia of Computer Science,* Van Nostrand Reinhold Co., 135 West 50 St., New York, NY 10020, 1980, 1523 pp.

Snow, C.P., "Science and the Advanced Society," in *Computers and Automation,* April 1966, publ. by Berkeley Enterprises, Inc., Newtonville, MA 02160.

Susskind, Charles, *Understanding Technology,* Johns Hopkins University Press, Baltimore, MD, 1973, 163 pp.

Swain, Philip W., "Giving Power to Words," in *American Journal of Physics,* vol. 13, no. 5, October 1945, pp. 318–320.

Thomson, Sir George Paget, *The Foreseeable Future,* Cambridge University Press, New York, NY, 1955, 166 pp.

Thorndike, Edward L., and Irving Lorge, *The Teacher's Word Book of 30,000 Words,* Bureau of Publications of Teachers College, Columbia University, New York, NY, 1944.

Weeks, Raymond, *The Boys' Own Arith-metic*, E.P. Dutton & Co., New York, NY, 1924, 188 pp.

Witham, Joan, editor, *The SoftSide Sampler of TRS-80 Entertainment Pro-grams*, Hayden Book Co., Rochelle Park, NJ, 1982, 119 pp.

See also statements about "Source" or "Reference" at the end of lists.

Part 2

> "All the world's a stage,
> And all the men and women merely players;
> They have their exits and their entrances;
> And one man in his time plays many parts,
> His acts being seven ages....
> —*Shakespeare, "As You Like It," 1599*

This book has mainly resulted from my experiences in more than sixty years of activities. My list of occupations, avocations and roles played is shown below:

17(?) ROLES BY ACTOR ECB

(1) Begun (Continuing to)	(2) Occupation, Avocation, or Role	(3) Comments
1918(–p)	apprentice (gardener, naturalist, botanist, mineralogist, scientist, mathematician, story-teller)	planted potatoes in a victory garden; picked up jasper, quartzite, bloodstones;....
1920(–1982)	tourist, traveler	taken to France and England via ocean liner for summer, 1920;...have visited Australia, Hong Kong,..., 26 countries
1923(–1925)	member, president, chairman in a student society; secretary in another society	Phillips Exeter Academy, Exeter, NH
1926(–1981)	hiker, camper, mountain climber (low mountains)	White Mts., NH; Green Mts., VT;...
1926(–1929)	member, president, debater in a student society	Harvard Liberal Club, Cambridge, MA
1930(–1948)	employee, clerk, actuarial student, methods analyst, research consultant	two life insurance companies, New York, NY; Newark, NJ

1934(–p)	husband, father, stepfather, grandfather	6 children, 3 grandchildren so far
1935(–p)	writer, author, lecturer, poet	15 books; over 100 papers and articles; some 60 poems (not very good)
1942(–1946)	lieutenant (j.g.), lieutenant, lieutenant commander (U.S.N.R. on active duty)	dry land duty in U.S.A. (poor eyes)
1944(–p)	operator of one maxicomputer, 2 minicomputers, 5 microcomputers	never a good operator
1948(–p)	consultant, actuary, computer "expert"	clients few and far between
1949(–p)	president, one of the directors, chief executive officer, salesman, manager, file clerk, typist, emptier of waste baskets	the same small business always; one bank loan only, all repaid
1950(–1965)	constructor of a small complete mechanical brain (Simon), designer of small robots, scientific kits, computer software, holder of 2 patents	"Simon," front cover of *Scientific American*, Nov. 1950; "Squee," robot squirrel, front cover of *Radio Electronics*, Oct. 1951;...
1951(–p)	editor and publisher of *Computers and People* (formerly *Computers and Automation*) and other periodicals and publications	fascinating task, with no boss except the economic system
1952(–1960)	director, administrator, teacher in a correspondence school	over 1000 students worldwide eventually
1961(–1970)	employee, computer programmer, software designer, senior scientist	computer firm organized in 1961
1977(–p)	annuitant under Social Security	two strikes (= two small strokes) but not yet out

As a result of these various activities and occupations, as time went by, I found it necessary to publish quickly a number of short reports and booklets when they were needed for some purpose. For example, the correspondence school activity led to short publications on Boolean algebra and symbolic logic. And the production of a scientific kit on probability and statistics (which eventually sold more than 30,000 copies) inspired the publication of a short book "Probability and Statistics: An Introduction Through Experiments." Since we were already publishing in those years the magazine "Computers and Automation" (subsequently "Computers and People") and from time to time reprints from it, it was easy to publish reports quickly, and not wait for composing of a regular book.

References

In the following bibliographical listing, the following abbreviations are often used:

ECB Edmund C. Berkeley

ECB & A Edmund C. Berkeley and Associates, 36 West 11 St., New York, NY 10011, 1950 to 1954

Berk Ent Berkeley Enterprises Inc., 815 Washington St., Newtonville, MA 02160, 1955 to the present

p the present

CHAPTERS 1-6

Giant Brains, or Machines that Think, by ECB, publ. by John Wiley and Sons, New York, NY, 1949, 277 pp; second edition, 1961; translated into French.

Computers and People (magazine), formerly *Computers and Automation* (to 1974), ECB, editor, publ. by ECB & A, then Berk Ent, 327 issues, 1951–p.

The Computer Directory and Buyer's Guide (a special issue of *Computers and People,* formerly *Computers and Automation*), ECB, editor, publ. by Berk Ent, 26 volumes, 1955–p.

Computers — Their Operation and Applications, by ECB, publ. by Reinhold Publishing Co., New York, NY, eleven printings, 1956–66, 366 pp.

The Computer Revolution, by ECB, publ. by Doubleday & Co., New York, NY, 1962, 249 pp; translated into Japanese and Polish.

The Notebook on Common Sense, by ECB, publ. by Berk Ent, 100 issues, 220 pp., 1971–78.

Ride the East Wind: Parables of Yesterday and Today, by ECB, publ. by Quadrangle/The New York Times Book Co., New York, NY, 1973, 224 pp.

CHAPTER 7

How to Explain Clearly, by ECB, publ. by Berk Ent, 2nd printing, 1959, 24 pp.

Computer-Assisted Explanation, by ECB, publ. by Information International Inc., Boston, MA, 1967, 280 pp; available from Berk Ent.

CHAPTER 8

Construction Plans for SIMON; a Small Complete Mechanical Brain, 39 Pounds, by Edmund C. Berkeley and Robert A. Jensen, publ. by ECB & A, 2nd printing, Oct. 1952, 52 pp.

Squee, the Robot Squirrel — Construction Plans, by Edmund C. Berkeley and Jack

Koff, publ. by ECB & A, 2nd printing, August 1952, 22 pp.

The Construction of Living Robots, by ECB, publ. by Berk Ent, 2nd edition, 1956, 32 pp.

Small Robots: Report, by ECB, publ. by Berk Ent, 1956, 8 pp.

Constructing Electric Brains, by Edmund C. Berkeley and Robert A. Jensen, 3rd edition, 1957, 40 pp; reprinted from a series of 13 articles in *Radio Electronics*, 1950–1951.

Brainiacs — 201 Small Electric Brain Machines and How to Make Them, by ECB, publ. by Berk Ent, 1959, 256 pp.

The Programming Language LISP: Its Operation and Applications, by Edmund C. Berkeley and Daniel G. Bobrow, editors, and 15 authors; publ. by Information International Inc., Boston, MA, 1964, 392 pp; ECB was author of one article in book, "LISP — A Simple Introduction," pp. 1–49; reprinted by MIT Press, Cambridge, MA.

Computer-Assisted Documentation of Computer Programs, volume 1, by ECB, publ. by Information International Inc., Boston, MA, 1969, 120 pp; available from Berk Ent.

Computer-Assisted Documentation of Computer Programs, volume 2, by ECB, publ. by Berk Ent, 1971, 104 pp.

CHAPTER 9

Spelling — A Common Sense Guide, by ECB, publ. by ECB & A, 28 pp, 1952.

Letters for Fun: Helping Teach Your Children to Read for Fun — A Guide for Parents, by ECB, publ. by Berk Ent, 1956, 36 pp.

101 Maximdijes — Short Easy Cryptograms with Maxims for Answers, by ECB, publ. by Berk Ent, 1976, 32 pp.

CHAPTER 10

Strategy in Chess, by ECB, publ. by Berk Ent, 1952, 1 pp.

Numbles: Number Puzzles for Nimble Minds, by ECB, publ. by Berk Ent, 1954, 32 pp.

A Guide to Mathematics for the Intelligent Non-Mathematician, by ECB, publ. by Simon and Schuster, New York, NY, 1967, 352 pp., translated into Japanese and Swedish.

CHAPTER 11

Boolean Algebra (The Technique for Manipulating AND, OR, NOT and Conditions) and Applications to Insurance, by ECB, publ. by ECB & A, 1955, 56 pp, reprinted from the *Record of the Amer. Inst. of Actuaries*, 1937–38

The Relations between Symbolic Logic and Large-Scale Calculating Machines, by ECB, publ. by ECB & A; reprinted from *Science*, Oct. 6, 1950, pp. 395–399.

Circuit Algebra — Introduction, by ECB, publ. by ECB & A, 1955, 36 pp.

Symbolic Logic: Twenty Problems and Solutions, by ECB, publ. by ECB & A, 2nd printing, 1955, 32 pp.

A Summary of Symbolic Logic and Its Practical Applications, by ECB, publ. by Berk Ent, 4th printing, 1957, 28 pp.

Symbolic Logic and Intelligent Machines, by ECB, publ. by Reinhold Publishing Corp., New York, NY, 1959, 203 pp., reprinted by Berk Ent; translated into Russian.

CHAPTER 12

Probability and Statistics — An Introduction Through Experiments, by ECB, publ. by Science Materials Center, New York, NY, 1961, 140 pp; fifth printing, by Berk Ent, 1974; translated into French.

A Summary of Probability Distributions, by ECB, publ. by Berk Ent, 3rd printing, 1959, 24 pp.

CHAPTER 13

Glossary of Terms in Computers and Data Processing, by Edmund C. Berkeley and Linda L. Lovett, publ. by Berk Ent, 5th edition, 1960, 96 pp.

Teaching Machines, Programmed Learning, and Automatic Teaching Computers, by ECB, publ. by Berk Ent, 1963, 204 pp.

Studying by Yourself, by ECB, publ. by Berk Ent, 5th printing, 1966, 6 pp.

Index

The purpose of this index is to make the information in this book as accessible as possible. Before one first searches for a topic, a minute or two should be devoted to finding out how this index is organized and arranged.

Part 1: Names of Persons and Pseudo-persons

This part of the index contains names of persons like "Anthony Ralston"; pseudonyms like "Lewis Carroll"; fictitious persons like "Ignatius Trott"; legendary persons like "Prometheus"; and personalized animals like "Mah".

Russell, Bertrand, 46, 65, 111, 131
Russell, John B., 2

Safford, Herbert B., 3
Sammet, Jean E., 2
Schlesinger, Stewart, 5
Schmitz, Gerald C., 4
Schulman, Richard D., 4

Schultz, Claire K., 2
Shakespeare, William, 65
Sharpless, T. Kite, 8
Sherrod, John, 2
Shirley, Robin, 76

Simmons, D., 4
Skinner, B.F., 129
Smith, Caby C., 4
Smith, M., 4
Smith, Sam, 112

Snow, C.P., 1
Sophar, Gerald J., 2
Spuck, Dennis W., 3
Stanton, Jack, 4
Stolberg, O.E., 4

Sullivan, John W., 3
Susskind, Charles, 135, 136
Sutton, James B., 3
Swain, Philip W., 52
Swearingen, John K., 3

Tanaka, R.I., 4
Tanner, Verne H., Jr., 4
Tate, Vernon D., 1

Taylor, Paul W., 2
Taylor, Robert S., 2

Thompson, Mr., of Yell County, 90
Thomson, Sir George Paget, 101
Thorndike, Edward L., 87
Tighe, Ruth L., 2
Trott, Ignatius, 90

Turing, Alan M., 6
Turner, J. Crawford, Jr., 3
Tze, Lao, 46

Ulbrich, Erwin A., 5
Uncapher, K.W., 4

Van Dusseldorp, Ralph, 3
Venn, John, 109
Voltaire, 65
Vorlander, Carl, 4

Wagner, Gerald E., 5
Ware, Willis H., 4
Warnke, D.H., 3
Weitz, Russell, 3
White, Herbert S., 2

Whittier, C. Taylor, 3
Wiener, Norbert, 6
Will, Daniel A., 3
Williams, Samuel B., 2
Wilson, James J., 4

Wolle, James E., 5
Wood, Merle, 5

Yarbrough, Everett, 3
Yau, S.S., 4

Part 2: References to Alphabetical Lists

This part of the index consists of some cross-references to lists which are alphabetically sequenced.

For computer magazines, see the alphabetical list by title of computer magazine in Chapter 3, pages 14 to 25.

For computer societies of several kinds, see the alphabetical lists in Chapter 2, pages 8 to 13.

For reserve or key words of the programming language CBASIC, see the alphabetical list on pages 59 to 62.

For reserve or key words of the programming language COBOL, see the alphabetical list on pages 56 to 59.

Part 3: Names of Principles for Solving Problems

This part of the index consists of an alphabetic list of 49 names of principles for solving problems. For each name X, "The Principle of X" should be understood. For example, "The Principle of Mr. Micawber" (which is "Something will turn up.") All the principles are inventoried on pages 93 to 95.

Part 4: Names of Fallacies

This part of the index consists of an alphabetic list of 38 names of fallacies in reasoning. For example, the fallacy of the "Leading Question" is illustrated in

"Do you still beat your wife, yes or no?" The fallacies are inventoried on pages 110 to 112.

Part 5: Subjects and Topics in General

This part of the index contains: the names of subjects and topics in general; words, phrases, sometimes sentences; names of places, countries, peoples, societies; some condensed titles of lists; and so on.

often, 113
On-Off Circuit Elements, 106
1, one, 85
OP (operation), 105
operation, 27, 105
Opossum Eating Persimmons, 91
output, 27

Pancakes, 91
parent, 100
PASCAL, 56
Pascal's Distribution, 118
Patagonia, xi
patterns of distributions of probability,
    118
patterns of events, 118
Pavan for the Children of Deep Space, 78
pawns, 96
pen and sword, xii
pencil and paper, 53, 133
people in a computer system, 45
periodic table, 26
peripherals, 27
Persimmons, 91
personal computers, 98
physical reality, 113
pig-headed, 111
PL/I, 56
+, plus sign, 105
poems, 76 to 81
Poisson Distribution, 118
pollution of the environment, 133
Polya's Distribution, 118
Pompeii, 127
population explosion, 132
predicates, 108
primate brain, xiii
prime number, 92
principle of mass production, 102
Principles for Solving Problems, 93
Principles for Solving Problems in Office
    Operations, 94
Principles for Speaking, Explaining,
    Arguing, and Persuading, 52
probability, 113, 118
probability weighing, 73
Problems for Students of Algorithms and
    Programming, 55

Problems in Arithmetic for Supple
    Minds, 90
procedure, 27
process, 130
processing, 27
program, 27
programming languages, 56
propaganda, 133
proposition, 101, 107
Propositions Regarding Language,
    Communications, and Intelligence,
    75
Propositions Relating to Input,
    Processing, and Output, 46
public relations expert, 109
punch card, xiii
Pythagoreans, 85

quantum theory, 102

rabbit hunting, 90
reading machine, 130
realities of a situation, 108
reasoning, 27
Reasons for Refusing Job Offers, 36
Recognition Technologies Users
    Association, 4
recognizing machine, 130
reflection, age of, 97
regions, 107
reserve words of CBASIC, 59-63
reserve words of COBOL, 56-59
riddles which the world propounds, 81
risks, 114
robots, xiii, 130
Romans, 132
Russia, 111

scholar, xix
science, 134
shipwreck, 114
skin of a computer system, 66
silly science, 134
simulation, 126
slash, xvi
slide rule, 5
smelling smoke, 98
Society of Data Educators, 5
Society for Computer Simulation, 5

Part 6: The Future

What about the future? More information of the kind contained in this book (lists of topics related in one way or another to computers and related subjects) has been and will be published in the department *CACBOL* of the magazine *Computers and People*, in issues that have gone or will go to press after about mid-1983. This was the approximate date of release of the manuscript for this book to the publisher, Issues of 1984 (Volume 33), 1985 (Volume 34), 1986 (Volume 35), and so on will contain many more installments.

These issues may be obtained by subscription ordered from Berkeley Enterprises Inc., 815 Washington St., Newtonville, Mass. 02160, U.S.A., at the price in effect when the order is mailed.

Also, the issues may be consulted at many libraries: public libraries; libraries at colleges, universities, high schools, technical institutes; libraries at large corporations and businesses. A brief indication of the density of paid subscriptions that go to libraries is as follows:

Area	Number
Ohio	95
Norway	12
Japan	72
Australia	50